T0277860

A Man and His Home
Ralph Dutton of Hinton Ampner,
8th Baron Sherborne

A MAN AND HIS HOME

Ralph Dutton
of Hinton Ampner,
8th Baron Sherborne

JOHN HOLDEN

PALLAS ATHENE

SERVABO FIDEM

Ralph Stawell Dutton
of Hinton Ampner House, Hampshire

Ralph Dutton's bookplate

CONTENTS

For Alexy

Acknowledgements

I became interested in writing a life of Ralph Dutton when I discovered, to my surprise, that there was no existing biography. My first step was to contact the National Trust who own the estate and house at Hinton Ampner, and they have provided invaluable help by opening their archive, and Hinton Ampner itself, to my researches. In particular, this book would never have seen the light of day without continuous support from Rebecca Wallis of the National Trust, and I thank her most heartily for being a source of advice, information and encouragement.

I would also like to thank the staff and volunteers at Hinton Ampner and at the National Trust archive in Micheldever Station. Hampshire Archives in Winchester facilitated access to Ralph Dutton's papers during the Covid lockdown, and the archivists of Christ Church, Oxford, and the Wallace Collection also deserve thanks for their assistance.

Ralph Dutton's godson, Henry Legge, and the former director of the National Trust, Martin Drury, both gave me their vivid memories of meeting the subject of this book, and I wish to thank them for their enlightening and thoroughly enjoyable conversations.

R. C. Richardson, emeritus professor at the University of Winchester, deserves a special mention. His essay on Ralph Dutton and 'Englishness' (details of which can be found in the bibliography) provided a springboard and an inspiration for my own work.

Seeking permission to use photographs can be a difficult issue for authors, especially when the images are old and of uncertain origin. I am pleased to say that everyone I contacted was exceptionally helpful. Special mentions go to Mirabel Cecil, Lucinda Webb at Portsmouth High School GDST, the churchwardens of All Saints, Hinton Hill, Clare Hastings, Martin Yeoman, the staff of National Trust Images, and to Derry Moore, who gave permission to use his wonderful image of Ralph Dutton in the garden of Hinton Ampner on the cover. I would also like to thank the publisher of this book, Alexander Fyjis-Walker, and the editor, Caroline Brooke Johnson, for their encouragement, expertise and diligence.

Several people read early drafts and chapters of this book and provided useful comments, among them Jerzy Kierkuć-Bieliński, Charles Tharp and Jean Bright, but the main burden of reading and re-reading fell on my friend and frequent collaborator Robert Hewison. As ever, I cannot thank him enough for taking the time and trouble involved in the task. All errors and omissions of course remain entirely my own.

Note on sources and terms

Rather than interrupt the flow of this book with footnotes, I have included sources and a wider bibliography in a list at the end. I have endeavoured to clarify all sources, both written and oral, within the text, but if the source of any quotation is unclear I apologise to its originator. If anything is obscure, I will be happy to respond to any reader's enquiries.

Every effort has been made to contact the correct copyright owners of the images, and to obtain their permission. If any errors or omissions have been made, apologies are offered, and any mistakes that are notified to the author will be rectified in any future reprints or editions of this book.

Throughout this book I have used the word homosexual to describe men and women who have same-sex attraction or orientation. Nowadays it would be more usual to use the term gay, but homosexual is the word that Ralph Dutton and his circle would have used, and I decided to employ the language of their day rather than the nomenclature of our own. The word homosexuality is now considered to be a legal and medical term – as indeed it was in Ralph's time – with all that that implies.

Ralph Dutton of Hinton Ampner:
A Man and His Home

> At last an obit. of dear old Ralph Dutton who died a week ago.
> Such a sweet man. I shall always remember his deep-throated
> laugh of three *her-her-hers*, and much twinkling of those lit-
> tle pig eyes. He was exceptionally ugly, with a large nose. As
> a youth he must have been singularly unattractive physically,
> but always redeemed by his niceness and charm [...] A cor-
> rect, patrician sort of man, always full of anecdotes and very
> cultivated. One of the last Edwardians of that school.

This was what James Lees-Milne, friend of Ralph Dutton and
long-time servant of the National Trust, recorded in his diary for
26 April 1985.

Lees-Milne's nugget leaves us wanting more, and yet there is
no biography of Ralph Dutton, no entry in the *Dictionary of National Biography*, and he never had his portrait painted: 'my face is
not my fortune,' he said.

Ralph Dutton is elusive, but he is worthy of our attention for
two reasons. First, because he created something remarkable:
Hinton Ampner in Hampshire, an estate, garden, house and contents that give great æsthetic pleasure to visitors today, and which,
when he was alive, were the setting for the pursuit of a particular type of *douceur de vivre*. Ralph Dutton looked backwards to
eighteenth-century classicism and the rural patrician tradition,
and forwards to modern domestic comforts and public access. In
his hands, Hinton became an elegant setting for living 'the good

Hinton Ampner today

life', one that brought together friendship, food and wine, rooms and gardens, intellectual endeavour and public benevolence.

The creation of Hinton elevates Ralph Dutton above the ordinary, and he did it not once, but twice. As the *Sunday Times* literary critic Raymond Mortimer put it, writing about Ralph's second rebuilding of Hinton in 1960:

> By then he was over 60, and a bachelor without even a nephew or a niece. To many [...] his enterprise may seem an anachronism, even an absurdity. In my view it was magnificent, and might have inspired a story by Balzac or Henry James [...] Dutton's ruling passion, one gathers, is for beautifying his house, garden and park. To that he has devoted his life, as others to composing poetry or music. Anyone thus obsessed is exceptional and I think interesting.

The second reason why Dutton deserves our attention is because of his role as an enthusiast for eighteenth-century architecture and decoration. He formed part of small patrician group who through scholarship, public service and investment of their own funds did a great deal to conserve English country houses at a time when they were being demolished at an alarming rate. The tastes of Ralph and his friends came to influence the decisions of cultural institutions, and from there to affect public attitudes to heritage.

Ralph Dutton's role as the creator of Hinton is now seen as seminal by the National Trust. In their *Statement of Significance* (a document written when a property is acquired), they say of Hinton:

> In the context of the whole property, it is more important to view the acquisition not as a sum of individual parts, but as a representation of the vision of one man and his quest for tranquility in a time of great upheaval [...]. Hinton Ampner's character is inextricably linked with the man who initiated everything that the Trust now holds.

The physical evidence of Hinton is clear for all to see—wide views, extensive gardens, fine rooms—but the man behind it is a mystery. In spite of his wide acquaintance, he features only fleetingly in the diaries and letters of his contemporaries. Even his entry in *Who's Who* is short and unrevealing. He was a shy and reticent man who led a privileged life that followed a conventional course: Eton, Christ Church, travel and the Foreign Office, scholarship, committee work and local benevolence.

As one of his close Hampshire friends commented: 'In spite of his open, friendly manner, Ralph remained a private man. You could know him for years and not know him. A bold trespasser would soon encounter a wall he could not climb or a notice marked "Private".'

It is time to climb over that wall to find out more about Ralph Dutton, the man who created Hinton Ampner.

*Hampshire in c. 1810: Hinton Ampner to the top right,
to the east of Winchester*

Chapter One:
1898-1912

Ralph (pronounced 'Rafe') Stawell Dutton was born on Thursday, 25 August 1898 at Hinton Ampner House, which lies about nine miles east of Winchester in Hampshire. He died after falling down the main staircase in the same house almost eighty-seven years later, on Saturday 20 April 1985. For the last three years of his life, he was known as the 8th (and last) Lord Sherborne, having inherited the title (but nothing else) from a cousin.

In later life, Ralph was to become interested in genealogy and traced his origins back through Lord Sherborne and Lord Stawell to sixteenth-century origins in Somerset. Along the way bloodline connections were formed with the Curzon and Bilson-Legge families, grand houses were acquired (including the very grand Sherborne House) and riches accumulated.

Ralph's grandparents, John Thomas Dutton and his wife Lavinia, began living at Hinton, which was a family property through the female line, in 1857. Their son, Ralph's father Henry John Dutton was ten years old at the time. The leasehold of the property, held from the Bishopric of Winchester since the mid-sixteenth century, was turned into a freehold in 1863. At that point, Ralph's grandparents began to plan, and then to build afresh, in order to replace the unfashionable Georgian box of Hinton Ampner House with something more up-to-date. The result was very definitely *not* to Ralph's taste. Commenting on the builder, he says that:

Hinton Ampner: the house built by Ralph Dutton's grandfather

Mr Kemp, of Alton, [...] had erected a number of particularly hideous buildings in the neighbourhood. Purely as a
builder there was nothing amiss with his work; as a planner
and designer his ignorance was abysmal, and I fear I should
add that my grandparents cannot have been much better.

It was this house, a 'monstrosity' in Ralph's view, together with
the estate and other properties, that passed to Ralph's father when
his grandfather John Thomas Dutton died in 1884.

Ralph's father, Henry John Dutton (1847–1935), had been living a quiet life at Hinton for about a decade before he inherited.
After serving for some years in the Rifle Brigade, he had retired
to Hampshire to look after the Hinton Ampner estate and the
nearby Hartley Mauditt estate, which he also owned. His life

was spent mostly shooting in winter—partridges at Hinton, and 'remarkably good' pheasant at Hartley Mauditt—and playing croquet in summer. According to Ralph, his father had 'no intention of marrying, and looked to his younger brother to carry on the line'. But when Henry John Dutton was thirty-nine, his younger brother died and he felt obliged to find a bride. The woman he chose was the twenty-year-old Blanche Cave. She was almost half his age and unlike him in both temperament and interests. There is no record of how they were introduced to each other, but the alliance of a monied bride with an old aristocratic lineage was no novelty.

Blanche's family was wealthy; the money came from banking in Bristol and, as with the Dutton family, there were also connections to plantations in Barbados. Unfortunately Blanche's grandfather was a miser, and her parents decided to live abroad in Florence where life was cheaper. The old man died in 1870, and the inheritance of roughly a million pounds changed everything; Blanche, aged three, returned to England with her family and her father Laurence Cave built a large country house for the family at Ditcham, about sixteen miles from Hinton. He also bought a town house in Lowndes Square in London and a steam yacht.

While the Cave family fortunes of Ralph's mother were waxing, those of his father, Henry John Dutton, were waning. The new house at Hinton had been built on the back of substantial agricultural rents, but a collapse in grain prices caused by the opening up of the American plains, cheap transportation, and the decision not to impose import tariffs on cereals led to a severe depression in the agricultural sector from the mid-1870s onwards. The result was summed up by Lady Bracknell, in Oscar Wilde's *The Importance of Being Earnest*:

What between the duties expected during one's lifetime, and

the duties exacted from one after one's death, land has ceased to be either a profit or a pleasure. It gives one position and prevents one from keeping it up. That's all that can be said about land.

Henry John Dutton married Blanche Cave in 1888, but despite her family's riches, his wife unfortunately brought with her less than he had been expecting. She received only half the settlement that her elder sister had been given on her marriage, and Ralph's parents had to wait until 1892, when Henry John's uncle died and left him properties in Timsbury and Bedhampton, before their fortunes recovered. In the meantime, although they were far from poor, Ralph's parents had to be careful.

For the first six years of their marriage, the couple were childless, so it was of no great consequence that Hinton had only one bathroom, two working lavatories and an inadequate water supply. There was no electricity either—a generator was not installed until 1913.

In 1894 the first of four children arrived. Blanche Mary Stukeley (1894–1976) was followed by Ursula Mary Lavinia (1896–1978). Then came Ralph in 1898 and finally Joane Mary (1902–1987).

Blanche's pregnancy with Ralph must have been uncomfortable, not only on account of the lack of facilities in the house, but also because of the weather. The summer of 1898 was exceptionally hot, and the August Bank Holiday that came on the Monday following Ralph's birth was marked by record numbers of people punished for drunkenness and fighting: it was in August 1898 that the word 'hooligan' first appeared in the newspapers.

Ralph's father was a keen reader of the press and no doubt followed these stories of social unrest with disapproval. Characteristically, however, when Ralph wishes to explain his father's personality, he talks not about politics but about interior decoration:

Henry John Dutton, father of Ralph Dutton

In keeping with my father's interests were a number of agreeable aquatints of famous horses, but dominating all else were three large oil paintings of his favourite dogs […] all through his life he very sensibly preferred his dogs to his children […]. On the left of the chimney breast was a bookcase containing the books one would expect. Surtees and Whyte-Melville, books on hunting and pugilism interspersed with a number of late Victorian and Edwardian autobiographies […]. Behind the chair was a glass-fronted case containing his most prized possessions—his guns.

The hall of Hinton Ampner as it was in Ralph Dutton's early years

By contrast, Ralph's mother's character was not stamped on Hinton in the same manner. She seems to have had little influence over how the house was decorated. Ralph himself says of his mother: 'Although she had a rather vivid personality, she in no way imparted this to her surroundings'; and she frequently referred to the place as 'this barracks of a house'. Yet Blanche was neither dull nor unassertive. Charlotte Bonham-Carter (a public servant and art-lover who lived nearby in Alton) described her as 'the most elegant, lively, endearing, amusing and brilliant creature and so full of surprises [...] I feel she completely overshadowed Ralph who in his youth was quite swallowed up or buried among those three sisters.'

From Ralph's perspective in the nursery and the schoolroom, he remembered 'no pictures on the flowered wallpaper, nor indeed any single object of any beauty in the room which could have inspired the youthful mind'.

Against this 'gloomy aspect', he notes the 'dreary lives' of a succession of four German governesses who taught and looked after Ralph and his sisters before they went to school. The Fräuleins von Brandt, Mehrendorf, Bomark and Wedekind made no great mark on Ralph, although he was fond of the last of them. His mother, who spoke fluent German, would have been able to converse with them in their own language—before the First World War, royal family connections meant that English society looked to Germany, rather than France.

Ralph was an isolated child. He and his father had completely different interests; he and his mother had completely different personalities. With an unsympathetic and distant father and a loving but extrovert mother, together with two older sisters to whom he never seems to have been particularly close, his affections turned elsewhere, to his nurses. When he was in his early seventies, Ralph made some handwritten notes, possibly with a

Ralph Dutton as a young horseman, with his older sisters
Blanche and Ursula, c. 1904

view to writing his autobiography. It never went further than a few pages about his early years, but he has this to say:

> When I read childhood reminiscences the writers seem usually to have retained a clear memory of the domestics—if any—who surrounded them during their early years. My memories in this direction seem indefinite […]. Naturally the most important person in our childhood was our nurse.

Old Nana (who left after eight years' service when the German governesses arrived) and New Nana were central figures in Ralph's life. He was also fond of the butler, Burrows. Servants remained emotionally important: towards the end of his life Ralph walked down to nearby Cheriton almost every day to visit his retired housekeeper.

In the earliest years of the twentieth century, life at Hinton Ampner was settled and quiet. There was an annual routine of visits to Hartley Mauditt, where the family stayed at Groom Farm and where his father shot. Ralph's parents knew Groom Farm well—they had lived there briefly in 1894 when Hinton was let for six months to help with the finances—and it must have been a home-from-home: like Hinton, it had no bathroom. The WC arrangement was different, however, as the one at Groom Farm was a sociable affair that could be used by two people simultaneously. Although less than twenty miles from Hinton, Groom Farm was in a different terrain and it took all day to get there. At Groom Farm they enjoyed country walks and autumn sunshine. But it did not last long:

> For me these Arcadian visits to Groom Farm ended when I went to my preparatory school in 1907, but I think the other members of the family spent happy weeks there while I was endeavouring to forget the German I had learnt from the Governess and to replace it with Latin and French.

Ralph's father eventually sold the farm sometime around 1912.

In 1909 Ralph's mother bought a twin-cylinder Darracq—a model that later found fame in the title role of the 1954 film *Genevieve*. Blanche had a few lessons driving round and round Belgrave Square, after which she felt sufficiently confident to attempt short distances in the country. She frequently drove to Winchester, accompanied by a chauffeur/groom who was there not to help with the driving, but to change the tyres when punctures occurred, as they frequently did on the untarmacked flinty roads.

It was in the Darracq that Ralph and his mother went to visit cousins in Gloucestershire, probably in 1909. The trip is significant because Ralph's record of it shows that he was already interested in buildings as a child, and moreover had already acquired a vocabulary to record architectural details. He also encountered some splendid interiors in the great houses that he visited.

Blanche drove, Ralph sat in the passenger seat and Tom the groom looked after them. Before the First World War, there were few cars on the roads—about 10,000 in 1909, compared

A 1905 four-cylinder Darracq tonneau

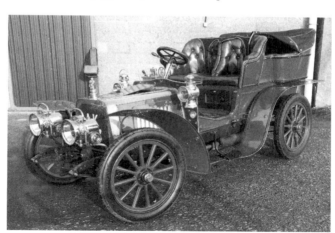

to 32,000,000 in 2020—and almost none of them was driven by a woman. Blanche was a pioneer, and the Duttons' progress through Hampshire and Wiltshire to Gloucestershire must have caused people to stop in the street.

On the first day they covered thirty miles and arrived safely in Salisbury, staying at the famous coaching inn, the White Hart. The second day involved a long drive of fifty miles to Tortworth Court, a large mansion near Thornbury in Gloucestershire, built between 1848 and 1853. This was the home of the 3rd Earl of Ducie, whose mother was Elizabeth Dutton, daughter of John Dutton, Ralph's great-grandfather.

The house was much larger and more impressive than Hinton and Ralph was somewhat over-awed:

> Dinner for me was an ordeal. I was very shy and there were quite a number of visitors staying in the house. I think we sat down about fourteen to dinner. It was all very grand indeed, six footmen in gorgeous liveries, gold plate to eat off and delicious food.

Writing up the visit sixty years later, Ralph reflected wryly that Tortworth had since been converted into an open prison, 'one of those up-to-date institutions for well-behaved malefactors'. The house in fact suffered an chequered history from the Second World War onwards, becoming first a naval training base, then HM Prison Leyhill and then a training school for prison officers. In 2001 it was rejuvenated as a hotel, which it remains to this day.

From Tortworth the party motored on to another Gloucester-shire mansion, Sherborne House, which 'was even more splendid'. As Ralph noted: 'My great-grandparents were extremely rich.' Their spectacular wealth resulted from the confluence of land in Gloucestershire belonging to Ralph's great-grandfather John Dutton, 2nd Lord Sherborne, and the 15,000 or so acres owned by the woman he married in 1803, Mary Bilson-Legge, popularly known as 'the Hampshire Heiress'.

Ralph's retrospective notes on his visit include detailed memories about the architecture and the contents, evidence of a keen interest in these subjects. Sherborne House had been remodelled in 1829–34 for John and Mary by Lewis Wyatt, a nephew of James Wyatt, with the principal interior rooms designed by Anthony Salvin around 1841. The house left the Dutton family in 1971 and was converted into flats in 1981. The park was donated to the National Trust in 1982 on the death of Charles Dutton, the 7th Baron Sherborne. While staying at Sherborne House, Ralph and his mother visited yet more Dutton properties—Bibury Court and Lodge Park (the latter is also now a National Trust property).

The difference in temperament between Ralph's father and mother played out not only in her enthusiasm for, and his aversion to, motor cars, but in their contrasting views about London. When Ralph was four years old, his mother began an annual practice of renting a property in town for the months of May and June, in other words the London Season: 'my father, never reluctant to be free of his family for a space, was persuaded to give financial support to this enterprise.'

The first year Blanche rented a house was 1902 and she chose a property in Clifford Street, just north of Piccadilly. In later years she rented in Belgravia's Chesham Place and Herbert Crescent, and finally in Eaton Place. Ralph traced his own love of London directly to his mother's influence: 'My mother had been largely brought up in London and she had a great affection for the place. It was not an affection my father shared, but it is one which I inherited.'

After the seclusion of Hinton, London offered many delights and diversions. There were visits to the Natural History Museum, to Hyde Park, and to McPherson's Gymnasium at 30 Sloane Street, where a young Harold Macmillan, who was four years older than Ralph and destined to be a fellow Etonian and future prime minister, exercised most days.

Ralph attended children's services at St Peter's Church in Eaton Square, but had no recollection of socialising with children or going to any parties. One day, when he was seven years old, he persuaded his governess to take him to visit the Wallace Collection. They were refused admission on account of his age. Later in life Ralph was to serve as a trustee of the Wallace Collection for more than twenty years.

When they returned from London to Hinton, Ralph could look forward to summer holidays, which were usually spent in Swanage in September. In 1910 they went instead to Bude, staying in the newly opened Grenville Hotel, designed by the architectural firm of Hatchard-Smith, whose work ranged from orphanages and workingmen's clubs to Dalston Junction Turkish Baths.

It was in Bude that something happened which Ralph recorded in detail sixty years later. He prefaces the account by saying that 'My childhood and indeed the greater part of my early life was on the whole free from anything which could properly be called a dramatic incident.' In Bude, however, his two older sisters faced serious danger. The event was reported in the *Cornish & Devon Post* on Saturday 10 September:

> On Monday two young ladies, visitors staying at the Grenville Hotel, Bude, had a narrow escape from being drowned. They were bathing and got carried out to sea. Great excitement prevailed among the people on the beach, and many willing helpers went to the rescue. A boat was, after a good deal of difficulty got out, and luckily it was in time to assist in bringing the girls to a place of safety. Had they for one moment lost their presence of mind they would undoubtedly have perished, for neither of them could swim. They floated

The Grenville Hotel, Bude, c. 1910

until help came, two visitors very pluckily going out in advance of the boat […] we are pleased to know that both the young ladies are very little the worse for their adventure.

After being educated at Hinton by German governesses, Ralph attended West Downs preparatory school in Winchester, starting there at some point in 1907. He makes only a passing reference to his prep school in the record of his childhood, but others speak of the place, which had been only recently established in 1897, as enlightened and interested in new educational ideas, such as those of Miss Charlotte Mason, who advocated a liberal education influenced by John Ruskin and Matthew Arnold. Norman MacMunn, who taught there during the First World War, described the school as being 'interested in the emancipation of the child'.

West Downs was Ralph's preparation for life at Eton, where most boys he encountered would have had a different sort of prior educational experience. Shane Leslie, an Irish diplomat who was a decade older than Ralph described his own, more conventional preparation for Eton as being a course in how 'to play football as honourably as the game of life, to recite the Kings of Judah and Israel, to love God and to hate Harrow'.

Chapter Two:
1912–1922

In the Lent (i.e. spring) term of 1912, 'Ralph Dutton of Hinton House, Alresford' started life at Eton College, where the headmaster was Edward Lyttelton, a first-class cricketer for both Cambridge University and the MCC. As well as being an impressive sportsman, Lyttelton was also deeply religious; he left Eton to become a curate to the Rev. Dick Sheppard who worked with the homeless at St Martin-in-the-Fields in London, before becoming rector of the parish of Sidestrand in Norfolk. Born into a prosperous, famous and large family (five of his seven brothers also played first-class cricket), and also handsome, religious and progressive, Lyttelton was an ideal candidate for the headmastership: 'As a cricketer and a vegetarian he was expected to satisfy the conservative as well as the advanced man.'

Ralph's housemaster at Eton was P. V. Broke, who was also a sportsman—he won the first golf tournament ever played at Burnham Beeches in 1891 and was the only player in that competition to complete a round in under 100—while Ralph's class tutor was C. H. Blakiston who in 1915 published *Elementary Civics*, a textbook on citizenship training.

When Ralph went to Eton in 1912 the United Kingdom was strong and confident. No age is free from anxieties, and between 1900 and the outbreak of war in 1914 the UK had to deal with many difficult and contentious issues of political and public concern, including Irish Home Rule, civic violence, the struggle for

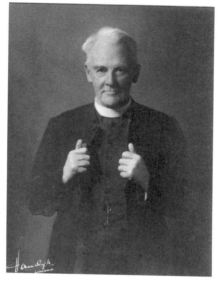

Edward Lyttleton, headmaster of Eton, 1905–1916

votes for women and trade union rights, a constitutional crisis between the House of Commons and the House of Lords, a transition of the monarchy from George V to Edward VII and the long-forgotten Agadir Crisis.

Nevertheless, there was a pervasive sense of natural, divinely purposed British superiority. The Delhi Durbar, often considered the zenith of the Empire's unsetting sun, took place in 1911, with George V in attendance confirming British power over the subcontinent. The British navy ruled the waves, and publications from *John Bull* to *The Times* via the *Daily Mail* extolled imperialism and the right of Britons to govern the world. It was a society marked by entitlement and self-belief.

Lord Grey of Fallodon, who was Foreign Secretary in 1912 (and who had a fishing lodge a few miles downstream from where the source of the Itchen River is found on the Hinton estate), had been told as a younger man by the colonialist Cecil Rhodes that 'you are an Englishman, and have subsequently drawn the greatest prize in the lottery of life'. If to be born English was lucky, then to be born English and also to go to Eton was to be at the very pinnacle of good fortune. Ralph's friend and fellow Etonian Osbert Sitwell later described the feeling: 'Life was a ripe peach and we were eating it.'

An Old Etonian writing during Ralph's time at the school sums up a common contemporary view:

> Eton invests boys with a social stamp entitling them to enter the free-masonry of English gentlemen [...]. The Etonian prefers graceful dignity to intellectual study [...]. The Headmaster of Eton has more to do with the soul of England than the Primate of Canterbury [...]. Eton taught little theology, moral or dogmatic. Decency and reverence were instilled instead [...]. In morals, Etonians have the Englishman's right to take their own line provided they do not become prigs on the one hand or beasts on the other [...]. Love of athletics made boys more Greek than Christian in their ideals.

Ralph's education at his prep school and then at Eton instilled in him the virtues of public service, fair play, civic responsibility, kindness and generosity, but also a sense of his own superior position in society and in the world more generally. Both schools also nurtured and confirmed his interest in the arts.

Ralph had a solid career at Eton. His sporting record shows him progressing from rowing in a four in June 1915 to a novice eight (*Dreadnought*) later in the year, and then graduating to an Upper Boat in 1917. It is likely that one reason Ralph became a 'wet-bob' was because of his poor eyesight, a serious problem that was to trouble him all his life and which made it impossible for him to excel at ball games, hence his lack of interest in them. Although he appears not to have gained any great academic honours and to have won no prizes, Ralph did in his last year become Captain of House, a position of significant authority and trust. Ralph's mastery of French, German and possibly Italian began in his school years, building on what he had learned from his German governesses. At Eton he concentrated on learning modern languages and travelled as well, probably in order to improve his language skills: a note made in 1930 refers to a trip he made to Brussels in 1914, just before the world was unexpectedly plunged into war.

Apart from study and sport, schoolboy life at the time had two other dominant themes: religion and sex. Ralph was not very interested in either, though, as we shall see in later chapters, there is more to be said on both subjects. When it came to sex, both at Eton and at Oxford there was a prevailing ethos of 'Greek' friendship between men, with the term covering everything from romantic but celibate admiration to illegal consummation.

The most important legacy of Ralph's time at Eton took the form of friendships that lasted a lifetime. Fifty years after leaving school, he was still in regular contact with Henry Studholme, one of his fellow oarsmen from the 1917 boat, who was also a contemporary at Oxford and who went with Ralph to New Zealand in 1927.

Another Eton friend was the writer and critic Sacheverell Sitwell and, in 1972, Ralph wrote this brief description of how they met, in response to a request from Denys Sutton, the editor of the art magazine *Apollo*:

> Sachie Sitwell is a few months older than I am, and went to Eton one or two halfs [i.e. terms] before I did. We were in different houses, and I don't think we came across each other for some time. Later we seemed to move up the school together usually being in a rather low form of the various removes—Sachie owing to a lack of interest in the curriculum, and I owing to a lack of any ability. I doubt whether

Sacheverell (left) and Osbert Sitwell in 1925

he was ever considered a brilliant or even particularly prom-
ising pupil. The School Library however was where he came
into his own, and here on free afternoons he would hold in
the gallery a little court, which I occasionally was allowed
to join. I was always amazed by his erudition. To me who
knew nothing, the breadth of his knowledge on a variety of
subjects seemed really astounding. Compulsory games were
one of the nightmares of school life, and during the winter
half there was an unpleasant form of football known as 'pick
up.' Boys who were not playing in any of their house teams
had to go down to the playing field at South Meadow and
there two of the more active boys would pick teams from the
available material. It was like a slave market and Sachie and I
were always the two left to the last. It was most humiliating.

One of Ralph's closest schoolfriends was Angus, Lord Holden.
He later became a British Liberal and then a Labour politician,
and served as speaker of the House of Lords in 1947. Ralph and
Angus Holden travelled together and co-authored two books,

Angus, Lord Holden

English Country Houses Open to the Public (1934) and *The Land of France* (1939). Like Ralph, Angus Holden was a bachelor all his life, but when he died at the age of fifty-one, it was less than a fortnight before the day appointed for his marriage with Mrs Charles Mackness, the widow of a soldier.

The sudden and untimely death of Lord Holden prompted Ralph to write an obituary for *The Times* which described him as:

> a man of vivid and genial personality who was known and loved in many circles. He possessed the gift of finding immense enjoyment in simple things, and amusement in the farcical and absurd [...]. It was impossible to be dull in his company, and his eagerness to listen to those with knowledge gave his conversation a warm and generous quality which brought the best out of many who were normally shy or silent.

Given his own shyness, Ralph must surely be referring to himself.
Another housemate at Eton was Christopher Hussey, who

*Christopher Hussey (1899–1970) in 1930,
medal by Robert Tait McKenzie*

became a noted architectural historian, writing frequently for *Country Life*. He served alongside Ralph on National Trust committees and became an enthusiastic advocate for all things Georgian and neo-Georgian. He died in 1970, aged seventy, and like Ralph, gave his house, Scotney Castle, to the National Trust.

Ralph left Eton in 1917 when he was eighteen years old and the country was still at war. He was unable to serve in the armed forces because of his poor eyesight and went instead to the Foreign Office where he spent two years as a clerk.

Ralph did not record his feelings about the war, but when he went up to Oxford in 1919, there must have been a stark contrast between those at the university who had served in the military and those who, on account of age or ability, had not. The hardened ex-soldiers were more self-confident. When Ralph arrived at Christ Church, his Eton contemporary and future Prime Minister Anthony Eden, had, by the age of nineteen, already earned the Military Cross for bravery in battle; he had also lost two of his brothers in the conflict. The writer Beverley Nichols, another Oxford contemporary who was president of the Oxford Union in Michaelmas Term 1920, and who would visit Hinton Ampner decades later, also had a military record and he had accumulated far more worldly experience than Ralph.

Entrance to Oxford University did not, in those days, involve fiercely competitive examinations and multiple interviews, though candidates did have to take an exam called responsions, known in student slang as 'Smalls', to demonstrate their competency. After the First World War, those who had undertaken military service were exempt from this requirement. In Ralph's case, his entry to Oxford was initiated by a letter from his mother and secured by two references from his Eton tutors. That was all it took.

The correspondence is remarkably brief and revealing, and started with Ralph's mother writing from Hinton House on 13 May 1919 to the Dean of Christ Church:

Dear Sir,

I am recommended by Mr Cuthbert Blakiston of Eton College to write to you to ask whether there would be a vacancy at Christ Church in October for my son, Ralph Stawell Dutton, Age 20½? [*sic*; she clearly did not know how old her son was]. He left Eton in Aug 1917, & being entirely rejected for the Army on account of his sight, he went into the Foreign Office. He is now leaving the F.O. because he wishes very much to go to Oxford. It is of course some time since he did any Latin & we are wondering whether F.O. work is equivalent to war service as regards exemption from Smalls? At Eton he specialised in Modern Languages during the last 2 years & did not take his school certificate. Mr Blakiston has kindly told me that he would give you my son's Eton record.

With apologies for troubling you,
Truly yrs
(Mrs) Blanche S Dutton

On 24 May Cuthbert Blakiston writes from Eton College:

My Dear Dean.

Thank you for your letter of the 20th: you of course gathered my attitude correctly. I am writing now on behalf of an old pupil, R. S. Dutton, whose work since summer 1917 has lain in the Foreign Office. He is most anxious to come up if possible to Christ Church & of course would be glad if his F. O. work should count as military service. He was rejected by every military board on account of bad sight & weak chest, though intelligent & useful. I have every wish to recommend him as he had a blameless career here & deserves a good Oxford education. His mother has I think written to you: she is a most excellent and able woman & one of the pillars of all good works in Hants. I hope to be in Oxford on Ascension Day & to call on you.

Yours ever,
Cuthbert Blakiston.

The recommendation from Ralph's housemaster is even briefer:

Gladwyns
Harlow
Essex

Oct 4 1919

Ralph S Dutton was in my house at Eton; his character throughout was without fault & he made a most excellent captain of the house in his last year (1916–17). Since he left he has been working at the Foreign Office. I can confidently recommend him to the Christ Church authorities.

P. V. Broke.

Apart from these letters, the Christ Church archive contains a record of 'Information desired in regard to a candidate for Matriculation at Christ Church.' In addition to administrative details such as Ralph's date of birth, the form asks 'To what work in life he is looking forward (if this is yet decided)?', to which Ralph's handwritten response is: 'Foreign Office or Diplomatic Service.' He also declares that there is no uncertainty about his intention of proceeding to his degree, although in the event, he left Oxford without attempting any examinations.

Ralph spent only two academic years at Oxford, from October 1919 to June 1921. He left no direct record of his experiences at Oxford, but it was a strange time to have been there. The First World War had disrupted the normal generational entry to the university so the variety of ages of the undergraduates was much greater than usual. There was the disparity between the school-boys who went straight from school to university, and the older generation who had served in the war. And there was also what might be called the presence of the missing—the brothers, friends and neighbours who should have been there to share the experience, but who had been killed. There must have been sadness, regret and survivor guilt, as well as an unbridgeable gap between those who had 'been there' and those who had not.

The 1920s are often thought of as a golden age at Oxford. The influence of Evelyn Waugh's *Brideshead Revisited* still casts a glow, or a shadow, depending on your point of view, over the decade, but the 'Brideshead generation', which included Harold Acton, Brian Howard, John Betjeman, Henry Yorke, Robert Byron, Cyril Connolly et al., and Evelyn Waugh himself, did not arrive in Oxford until 1922 or later. Many of them had been at Eton but had flourished there after Ralph had left, so Ralph's Eton was not Acton and Howard's Eton, and Ralph's Oxford was not Waugh's Oxford.

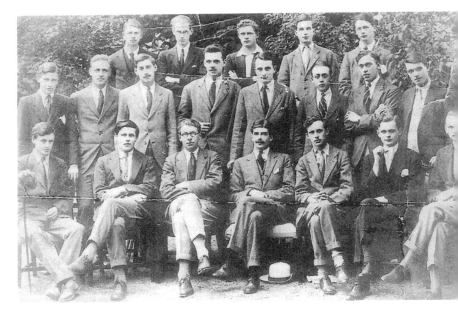

The Uffizi Society
Back row left to right: Lord Scone; Sir Walter Leslie Farrer; Eardley
Knollys; Roger Senhouse; Robert Gathorne-Hardy
Second row left to right: E. Fitzherbert ('Walter') Wright; W. Raeburn;
N. P. (or J.?) Kerslake; Henry Hope; Henry Studholme; Hon Edward
Sackville-West; Arthur Payne; Henry 'Chips' Channon
Front row left to right: J. Palmer; Lord Balniel; Ralph Dutton;
Anthony Eden; Lord David Cecil; T. Barnard; Angus Holden

A literal snapshot of Ralph's Oxford exists in the form of a photograph of the Uffizi Society, probably taken in 1921. The Uffizi Society was an art appreciation club where members read essays to each other and is an exemplar of how networks are formed. Of the twenty members, at least eight were Old Etonians, at least eight went to Christ Church, and in many cases their lives were entwined and their friendships persisted for decades.

A bespectacled Ralph is seated third from the left on the front row of the photograph, next to the Uffizi's founder, president and guiding light, the moustachioed Anthony Eden, who has been described as being 'a recluse, with a small circle of friends' at the time. The group formed an exclusive club so rarefied that it soon fizzled out because no-one was good enough to join them.

The members of the Uffizi Society were almost all wealthy and many were drawn from ancient landowning families. Three—Scone, Balniel and Cecil—already had titles of their own as undergraduates. Five of them were destined to become politicians with one, Eden, becoming Foreign Secretary and later Prime Minister. Another, Chips Channon, became a leading political diarist and introduced Ralph's friend and fellow Uffizi member Henry Studholme into Parliament in 1942. The careers of Eden, Channon and Studholme constantly rub up against each other, with Channon and Eden briefly overlapping at the Foreign Office and eventually becoming political enemies, and Studholme becoming a parliamentary whip under Eden's leadership.

Personal lives and careers are indistinguishable. In later life members of this group reviewed each other's books in national newspapers, served together on public bodies and became related by marriage: Lord David Cecil's elder sister Mary married the 10th Duke of Devonshire, while Lord Balniel married the third daughter of the younger brother of the 9th Duke of Devonshire.

These are the people that Ralph spent time with, associated with and conversed with. It was in this milieu that his attitudes and ideas, prejudices and views were formed. They are representative of their time and class and many of them went on to have extraordinary lives, involving public service, honours and significant achievements in their relevant fields. Several of the men in the photograph had successful professional careers. Sir Walter Leslie Farrer became solicitor to King George VI, Eddy Sackville-West became a noted music critic, and Lord David Cecil, a well-known academic and biographer.

Each of the Uffizi members was connected, through family or education, to other people of the same ilk, so that the network from this small group spreads outwards to friends of friends, sisters and brothers, cousins and colleagues, and as the decades unfold, the network developed, widened and became stronger.

As might be expected of the Uffizi members, they were united by a love of the arts and culture, and many pursued their interest into later life, with Lord Balniel serving as a trustee of Tate, the National Gallery, the British Museum, National Galleries of Scotland, the National Library of Scotland and the Royal Fine Arts Commission. He was also chairman of the National Trust from 1945 to 1965 where he overlapped with Ralph's service on various National Trust committees.

It is impossible not to notice how many of this group—at least eight—were homosexual or bisexual. According to John Betjeman, 'everyone was queer at Oxford in those days'. With homosexuality remaining illegal until 1967, these men dealt with their situation in different ways: some married, others formed more or less clandestine groups, but homosexuality was no bar to achieving financial and social success and public honours—at least if you were well-connected, discreet and wealthy.

Sometime in 1920, during Ralph's second year at Oxford, his father asked him how he was getting on at Cambridge. Perhaps feeling abashed, later that year he gave Ralph £10,000 (roughly £500,000 today), having sold 646 acres and several houses at the Kingsley estate in Somerset. According to Ralph's friend, the art historian Sir Brinsley Ford, this capital, which Ralph invested in the stock market 'enabled him to live very comfortably until the slump arrived in 1929'. The income from stocks and shares was supplemented in 1923 when Ralph became a Lloyd's underwriter (a passive role involving receiving an annual fee in return for taking on unlimited risk in the insurance market). He continued to be a Lloyd's 'name' for the rest of his life.

Having left Eton without taking the School Certificate and entered Oxford without taking the Responsions exam, Ralph left Christ Church, having studied Modern Languages but without taking a degree, in June 1921. At this point according to the historian R. C. Richardson, 'as a landowner in waiting, Dutton supplemented his academic studies with a more practical course at the Royal Agricultural College in Cirencester'.

By the time he was twenty-four years old, Ralph's lengthy, privileged but disjointed education came to an end without being completed. He was a well-connected young man with a network of friends, an interest in the arts, a command of four languages and a considerable income. He was also shy and reserved. His prep school and Eton had given him a sense of his self-worth and position in society, but also stressed the obligations of public service and the need to extend kindness and generosity to those less fortunate. Oxford had encouraged more serious scholarship and hard work, but must also have had a lighter side as friendships grew and Ralph and his peer group began to explore the world and what it offered.

In 1922 Ralph had no need to work and no interest in a career, but he was not prone to indolence. The question arose of what to do next while he waited to inherit Hinton with increasing impatience. The answer was to broaden his mind, extend his experience through travel and to cultivate the art of living as a cultured English gentleman.

Chapter Three:
1922–1930

By the early 1920s Ralph was a wealthy young man but not an idle one. He knew that at some point he would inherit Hinton and was eager to develop his knowledge and taste to fit himself for the role that he would play. Ralph tells us—in *A Hampshire Manor*, his book about Hinton written in 1968—that 'for a number of years before my father's death I had been considering how I could convert it into a house which I would find agreeable'. He was kept waiting for a long time, but he used that time productively.

Ralph's ideas were developed through study and by visiting a large number of buildings and collections both in the UK and abroad. Funded by his father's 1920 gift of £10,000 and his receipts as a Lloyds 'name', he could wander at will for extended periods. He became a regular traveller throughout his life, often in the company of a friend, usually with a cultural purpose and mostly within western Europe. But in November 1926, at the age of twenty-eight, he set off on an epic round-the-world voyage that lasted nine months.

His travelling companions on this trip were, for parts of the journey, Henry Studholme (who we have already met as a fellow oarsman at Eton and as a member of the Uffizi Society) and, for the entire trip, Hugh Cholmondeley. Hugh was a contemporary of Ralph at both Eton and Oxford where he went to New College. Unlike Ralph he was fit for military service, had joined the Coldstream Guards in 1917 and been awarded the Military Cross.

Ralph and Hugh were to travel together often in future years, usually departing from Le Pradet, a seaside town close to Toulon in the south of France where Hugh settled, at some point between 1922 and 1930, with an Italian companion named Carlo.

Ralph kept a detailed record of his round-the-world trip that took in New York, Washington DC, New Orleans, Veracruz, Mexico City, the Grand Canyon, Los Angeles, Stanford, San Francisco, Tahiti, New Zealand, Sydney, Brisbane, the Moluccas, Bali, Java, Sumatra, Singapore, Hong Kong, Kobe, Tokyo, Nara, Penang, Colombo, Socotra and Marseille.

There is much bathos in the diary, at times verging on the Pooterish: 'A coconut fell through the roof of our hut last night but luckily did not hit either of us', and, later, 'I shall thank God when we are off this boat.' There are also lofty judgements. At the first stop, New York, where they stayed at the Plaza Hotel: 'we are not very impressed by our first sight of the town.' Washington DC 'is not so fine as I had expected and has a curious provincial air', although the White House has 'charming Regency rooms'. New Orleans is 'rather charming, but I doubt we should think anything of it in Europe'.

In the United States he encountered some novel experiences, such as 'a self-service restaurant. The system is peculiar.' He and Hugh regularly found themselves taken up by friends of friends. In Los Angeles 'Elinor Glyn [the Romantic novelist] invited us to lunch. Tho' she must be 60 she is still a very good-looking woman […]. She took us to a movie-party; many stars there and all v. agreeable.'

After a hectic month in the US and Mexico, the trio set off by boat from San Francisco bound for Tahiti—'the hot days pass slowly'—and once there they had a wonderful time, the happiest of the whole trip, staying in a hotel converted from Gauguin's old house, relaxing on the beach, admiring the lush greenery—

and dodging coconuts. Despite being a long way from home, Ralph did not forget his familial duties and sent a telegram to his father at Hinton wishing him a happy eightieth birthday on 15 January 1927.

Ralph seems to have loosened up a little on the island:

> Tahiti is one of the few places in the world where one can live in esteemed respectability without either money or morals […]. After one day on the island I felt as much a part of it as the palm trees. It is a great refuge for those people who for one reason or another cannot live in their own country.

But he remained naïve: 'We crossed a river in which four young women were washing themselves. Greenshields [a tiresome Canadian fellow-guest at the hotel] stopped and photographed them but to our surprise they did not seem enormously pleased.'

After a blissful stay lasting three weeks, Ralph wrote: 'I am very sad at the thought of leaving', but the rainy season was beginning and New Zealand beckoned. At the shipping office a few days before their departure, Ralph met Evelyn Waugh's elder brother Alec, who was in distress and stuck, because a remittance had failed to arrive from England and he was unable to pay for his onward ticket. There is nothing to suggest that they had any previous connection, nevertheless Ralph there and then offered to lend Waugh £175 (equivalent to £7,500 today). Fortunately Waugh's money turned up in time and Ralph 'got the credit of a generous action without any of the bother'.

The boat trip to Wellington was uncomfortable and Ralph arrived with a bad earache: 'in great pain and a temperature'. It was sufficiently serious to land him in hospital for a couple of days and became a recurrent problem that brought on intermittent deafness and left him depressed. When he got out of hospital, he took a dim view of New Zealand:

Tahiti, c. 1922

I have never been to a country where the people are so plain and dreary in appearance and I think their outward looks are a true reflection of their minds. They are supremely unintelligent and provincial in their outlook but they are certainly very kind.

On leaving Wellington he comments: 'I was thankful to leave this windy and dusty town of hideous Gothic buildings and gimcrack wooden houses.'

From Wellington Ralph and his companions travelled to Christchurch, where they stayed with Henry Studholme's aunt and uncle, who appear to have been a rather stiff couple. Much to their disapproval, Ralph twice avoided going to church 'on the plea of my ear […] I wonder if my unorthodox views would have been thought a better or worse excuse than my ear? Anyhow I kept them to myself.' And that is all that he says on the matter of his religious opinions.

Henry and Ralph set out to tour both the north and south islands of New Zealand in a borrowed Riley, but the architecture did not improve. Napier was 'a shoddy little town' and 'Auckland another grim town […] less agreeable than Christchurch but not quite so bloody as Wellington.'

And then on, by ship, to Sydney, or 'Sidney' as Ralph insistently spells it. It was an unhappy voyage: 'Four of the worst days I have ever spent,' with a crowded boat and rough seas. But 'We like Sidney. It has many hideous buildings but there is a feeling of life about it. The inhabitants are far less bucolic than the New Zealanders and are really quite smart and many good-looking.' Ralph arrived when the Sydney harbour bridge was two years into its eight-year construction period, and he had reservations: 'It will be so immense that I feel it will throw the whole harbour out of proportion.'

Throughout his travels Ralph was always sensitive to whether a building's size and appearance, and the materials from which it was built, matched the landscape and the situation. As he said of Wellington: 'It is an excellent example of how a beautiful site can be ruined by unintelligent building.'

After calling in at Brisbane ('many big ugly buildings'), Ralph spent several days at sea and his thoughts went back to Hampshire: 'I have decided to write a history of Hinton when I get home. It really might be very interesting.' *A Hampshire Manor* was eventually published more than forty years later in 1968.

In early April 1927 Ralph reached the Moluccas where there was relief at last: 'nice old Dutch buildings […]. All rather smelly but picturesque.' On crossing the equator there was a party, with

'Everyone very frolicsome throwing about balloons etc. and free champagne and liqueurs were produced. These artificial high spirits always depress me.' Bali held echoes of the happy stay on Tahiti: 'The inhabitants of Bali [...] are partly Polynesian and rather good-looking. Neither men nor women wear anything above the waist. I am becoming quite an authority on bosoms!' As a reminder of how different travel was a hundred years ago, Ralph notes: 'there are no hotels in Bali and one has to stay in government rest houses which have 2 or 3 bedrooms. They are clean and adequate.' In 2023, Booking.com listed 9,704 hotels in Bali.

When he reached Surabaya, there was a hint of trouble ahead: 'There are rumours that the Japanese are mobilising to annex Manchuria. I pray this is not true.' It did not happen for another four years, and in the event did not stop him from continuing on through Java ('wonderfully beautiful and the food is universally good') and Sumatra to Singapore, and eventually to Japan itself.

After six months away from home, both Ralph and Hugh were developing homesickness. Ralph notes that 'It is 3 months since I have had any news from Hinton. Mother's last letter, which I got in Auckland, was dated Jan 16th.' On top of that, Singapore was a let-down after the sensory beauties of Indonesia: 'all is grim and businesslike' and Hugh was beginning to grate: 'We have had months of each other's company. This is distinctly too much [...]. I at any rate feel mentally quite dried up.'

Despite the continuing fears of war, they continued onward to Japan via Shanghai, which proved to be a brief but sociable stop. Henry Studholme reappeared, presumably en route home from New Zealand, and they met up with another acquaintance, David Keswick, who was part of the dynasty that ran the giant Asiatic trading company Jardine Matheson. David took them to the Shanghai Club, where they saw 'the longest bar in the world', then to the Country Club ('more cocktails') and then the French

Frank Lloyd Wright's Imperial Hotel Tokyo

Club ('still more cocktails') before dropping them off back at the boat at 1 a.m. Ralph enjoyed the cocktails (he retained a taste for them all his life) but disapproved of Henry who he thought 'most foolish to spend so much time bar-propping when he might be seeing interesting places'.

In Tokyo, Ralph's appreciation of good Modernist architecture is made clear by his reaction to Frank Lloyd Wright's earthquake-damaged Imperial Hotel, where he stayed: 'a great surprise, really a most attractive and interesting building.' He also appreciated 'the people who are very cheerful and attractive-looking. Some of the women with their kimonos are charming.' But his thoughts were never far from home, and he set about finding maple trees and dwarf thujas to send back to Hampshire for the garden at Hinton.

After three weeks in Japan, it was time to return to England, but given the political climate he decided that he would not travel home by train across Siberia and Europe but instead would take a boat all the way to Marseille. In spite of docking at Penang, Colombo, Socotra and Aden and traversing the Suez Canal, it was for him a long and tedious journey: 'My God how bored I am.' July 22nd 1927 was 'the last day on board—God be praised.'

When he finally got back to Hampshire, Ralph's mother was there to greet him on the platform at Winchester station: 'We had a most touching reunion. I'm delighted to be home.' Any disagreements with Hugh were forgotten:

> It is amazing how well Hugh and I got on together. Tho' we occasionally got a little short with one another in very hot weather we never had a single row, and there is certainly no-one else with whom I could have spent nine months without this occurring.

Ralph's final entry in the diary records the mileage between each stop and a calculation that he had travelled a total of 41,150 miles. There is also an *aide-memoire* noting that he had given his address to seven people, including Alec Waugh, the tiresome Canadian tourist Greenshields, and a sailor named Stanford.

Ralph's many travels in the 1920s and early 1930s suggest that he wanted to absent himself from Hinton. In his book *A Hampshire Manor* he reverses a quote from Edward Gibbon and says that he had passed 'some light and many heavy hours' there during his youth. He was also able to get away from Hinton by creating a life in London. Sometime in the late 1920s or early 1930s, he set himself up with a flat at 90 Piccadilly, ideally suited for a cultivated bachelor life since it was within easy walking distance of Savile Row (for his suits), Jermyn Street (shirts), St James's (his wine merchant, Berry Bros & Rudd), his club, Brooks's, the National Gallery and the Royal Opera House.

It is not known when Ralph moved into the Piccadilly flat, but it is mentioned in his travel diary for 1934 and there are photos

*'Vogue Regency' by Osbert Lancaster. Note the similarity to the
photograph on p. 71 of Dutton's London residence.
Both illustrations include a 'blackamoor' figure, common at the time,
but now widely considered as culturally insensitive or racist.*

from 1935. The rooms contain urns and statuary in hard stone—
one of Ralph's passions—and some good paintings, but the chairs
look uncomfortable, and in spite of the grandness of some individual pieces of furniture the overall effect is austere. In other words,
it appears that Ralph's ideas on decoration were still developing,
and that he was experimenting in a style that was relatively new
for the times—the Regency Revival—a style that was boosted in
1923 by the appearance of three articles in *House and Garden* which
'attempted to awaken a keener interest in the Regency'.

The cartoonist Osbert Lancaster dubbed the look 'Vogue Regency' in his illustrated history of interior decoration, *Homes Sweet
Homes*, where he astutely points out the historic parallel between

'the period between the Napoleonic wars and the upheavals of 1848, (and) the inter-war period [1918–39] in which vast social and political changes took place'.

He adds, writing in 1939, that 'To-day the more sensible of modern architects realise that the desperate attempt to find a contemporary style can only succeed if the search starts at the point where Soane left off.' Vogue Regency was not an attempt to recreate a period with historical accuracy, but rather a sensibility that sought to adapt the classical tradition to modern living conditions. It rejected heavy, ponderous and dusty Victorianism, and instead embraced a pared-back, light-hearted but considered and formal look. It rejected the radicalism of the Modern movement, but embraced central heating and cleanliness. It might be described as Modernism for conservative antiquarians.

Ralph was an early enthusiast for the eighteenth century. In the 1920s and 1930s there was a shift from what the architectural historian John Cornforth called 'The Cult of the Castle and the Manor House' to 'Augustan nostalgia and neo-Georgian Scholarship'. The writer Beverley Nichols said the same thing, but put it more whimsically:

> There comes a time, or there should come a time, in the life of every civilised man, when he realises that the eighteenth century said the last word worth saying in absolutely everything connected with the domestic arts […]. As it is with comfort so it is with taste; to linger in the Tudors is merely a sign of æsthetic adolescence.

Ralph became part of a triumvirate who embraced and promoted eighteenth-century style and created it in their own buildings and interiors. They were, as James Lees-Milne's biographer, Michael Bloch, writes: 'three close friends who, since the 1920s […] played a leading role both in "the Georgian Revival" and

The Dutton Family, a Conversation Piece, by John Zoffany

the movement to preserve country houses, the others being Christopher Hussey and Lord Gerry Wellesley.' Hussey, as we have seen, was a friend of Ralph's from his days at Eton. Wellesley, as we will see, was to be the architect for the reinvention of Hinton Ampner.

Another friend and Eton contemporary of Ralph's, Sacheverell Sitwell, was also a significant figure. He helped to organise a highly influential exhibition of eighteenth-century 'Conversation Pieces' in March 1930, hosted by the æsthete and politician Philip Sassoon in his home at 45 Park Lane, and Sitwell wrote a book with the same title, *Conversation Pieces,* that mentions two of Ralph's paintings. One of the paintings on display at the exhibition was *The Dutton Family* by Johan Zoffany, dating from 1771. Zoffany was a great traveller and at one point was shipwrecked off the Andaman Islands, where he and his fellow survivors stayed alive by eating a sailor. Zoffany's painting had left Ralph's family when it was sold by the 6th Lord Sherborne in 1929 and purchased by an American, Daniel Farr. It was sold again, to Lord Bearsted of Upton House, Warwickshire, whose descendants auctioned it in 2001, when it was bought by an unknown private collector. Ralph placed a reproduction of the painting on the wall of the dining room at Hinton Ampner.

Ralph's ideas about decoration and the eighteenth century were also influenced by his friendship with, and employment of, the interior decorator Ronald Fleming. Fleming, a Scot from Kelso who had served with gallantry and been wounded in the First World War, trained as a decorator in Paris in the early 1920s and was 'an enthusiast for the lightness of eighteenth century design'. When he lectured on the subject, he emphasised that decoration was very much a matter of personal and individual expression. According to the design historian Martin Battersby, he had been working in the Vogue Regency style since 1927 and may well have helped with the decoration of Ralph's flat at 90 Piccadilly.

Fleming lived for most of his adult life in an apartment in the house of the antique dealer (and owner of multiple country houses) Geoffrey Houghton-Brown at 20 Thurloe Square in Kensington. Fleming and Houghton-Brown are buried together in Putney Vale Cemetery in Wimbledon. In the 1950s, James Lees-Milne moved into the top floor with his new wife Alvilde.

When Ralph wrote Fleming's obituary for *The Times* in 1968, he said that

> his designs were on the whole conservative and for this reason have stood the test of time in a way that has not always been the case with the more avant-guard [*sic*] decorators. He had the gift, too, of introducing the owner's personality, rather than his own, into the rooms he created, so that they came to believe that the good taste they displayed was theirs, and hardly realised that they had been tactfully guided into the right path.

To return to Ralph's travels, at the end of July 1930 he set out on a two-month motoring tour of Germany, Austria, Switzerland, France, Belgium and the Netherlands with his friend Angus Holden. The initial leg of the journey took them by boat from Southampton to Bremerhaven and then by train to Bremen, where they headed to a wine cellar and tasted some 1726 Apostolen Hochheimer. If it was genuine it was a bargain—the equivalent of about 40p a glass—which is possible given the dire state of the German economy at the time. Regardless of the price, the pair judged the wine to be 'not very good'.

Next stop was Hamburg where they stayed at the Four Seasons, the best hotel in town, and went to visit the Reincke family. How Ralph met this family and exactly who they were is unknown, but they appear to have been excellent hosts and good company. Ralph commented that 'Herr Reincke is charming and everyone very agreeable', but typically he was more interested in their house, which he judged to be 'hideous'. On 13 July Ralph's car (for once he does not mention the make), which had been shipped over from England by Kuehne & Nagel, was delivered to his hotel, and he nervously got behind the wheel to motor to Lübeck with Lydia Reincke. With this successful day-trip completed, and after a 'superb dinner', he and Angus set off the next day for Berlin. Car journeys in those days were unpredictable and they broke down ten miles short of their destination, but were eventually able to have the condenser fixed and get to their hotel.

In Berlin they encountered a friend from England named in the diary as Francis Petre. This was in fact Francis Turville-Petre (1901–1941), a contemporary of Ralph's at Oxford and a member of an ancient, landed, Catholic family. In the mid-1920s Francis had been involved in a series of significant archæological excavations in the Middle East, but he had moved to Berlin in 1928, where, as an openly homosexual man he became friends with the

Nazis taking an interest in the books they were destroying
at the Institut für Sexualwissenschaft, 1933

writer Christopher Isherwood and the poet W. H. Auden. He features as a thinly disguised character in both writers' work.

Ralph and Angus met Francis in a *Biergarten* in Potsdam, but Francis was in the company of 'a troop of rather distressing friends, so Angus and I immediately left and returned to Berlin'. Why did Ralph find these friends so distressing? Was it their behaviour, their politics or their sexuality that provoked his reaction?

During his time in Berlin, Francis Petre worked and lived at the Institut für Sexualwissenschaft, commonly known as the Hirschfeld Institute after its founder Magnus Hirschfeld. Together, Francis and Magnus gave Ralph and Angus a tour of the building. Hirschfeld was an early campaigner for gay rights and the tolerance of homosexuality. He built a library on same-sex love and eroticism at the institute, which was burnt by the Nazis in May 1933. It is possible that Francis Petre had met Hirschfield, who he called 'Gusi', in 1929, when Hirschfield presided over the third International Congress of the World League for Sexual Reform which was held at the Wigmore Hall in London.

Ralph's comment on his visit to the institute is revealing: 'The "sexual data" is hugely interesting but quite nauseating and we left feeling faint and very pure.' We know that many of Ralph's close friends and acquaintances were homosexual or bisexual, and that throughout his education, both at school and at university, homosexual friendships were common. Ralph never reveals his own sexuality, so all comment on the matter is speculation. That said, we do know about Ralph's milieu and his character. He was shy and reticent, and found pleasure in all forms of culture, but particularly in the visual arts. What was important to him was the creation of Hinton, friendship, public service and scholarship. He was at ease in the company of homosexual men, but we know nothing about whether his friendships went further than that. He appreciated human beauty in both sexes and there are hints in his diaries of a romantic yearning for men, and possibly women. He never admitted to falling in love, and when it comes to the question of physical consummation, we have no information one way or the other. According to James Lees-Milne there was:

> No breath of his ever having had an affair of the heart. Yet he was, not admittedly in words, 'artistic'. All his intimate friends were so—Gerry Wellington with whom he travelled, and Geoffrey Houghton-Brown, with whom I last saw him when they lunched with us.

The writer Julian Barnes has written a study, *The Man in the Red Coat*, which deals in part with the life of the French æsthete and dandy Count Robert de Montesquiou (1855–1921). In it he comments:

That Montesquiou was homoerotic, that his passionate responses were all to men … is indubitable. His biographer Philippe Julian—no prude or moraliser—says that the Count grew to fear 'the impulses of the heart as much as the nonchalance of pleasure' […]. For such a Count, there might be something about pleasure (unless it is æsthetic pleasure) which could be grubby, open-ended, even middle-class. Fastidiousness is also the enemy of pleasure.

Could it be that for Ralph as well that fastidiousness was the enemy of sexual pleasure? The Berlin diary, written when he was thirty-one years old, suggests that he was interested, enquiring and appreciative of male and female beauty, but also prudish and not looking for erotic adventures. It is entirely possible that Ralph remained celibate all his life. He would certainly have thought any discussion of the matter impolite and in poor taste.

Chapter Four:
1930–1935

From Berlin, Ralph and Angus continued their 1930 tour by visiting the Bauhaus, the hugely influential and radical art and design school that had been set up in Weimar in 1919 and that had
moved to Dessau in 1925. Like the Hirschfield Institute, the Bauhaus was to be shut down by the Nazis in 1933. The school was
closed for a holiday and there was 'little going on', but Ralph was
shown round the 'huge white building in the modern manner' by
'a serious-minded student'. The visit shows Ralph being interested
in contemporary design as well as in history, appreciative of the
Modern when he considered it to be of good quality.

After Dessau, Bamberg:

> I shall always connect Bamberg with parties of young wom
> en singing. Every few minutes from 7 a.m. onwards, groups
> of girls with banners have been marching past the hotel and
> have much prejudiced my morning slumber. I can't imagine
> what they were doing.

The parties of flag-waving young women are likely to have been
involved in a political rally. Bamberg had been chosen by Hitler
to host a conference in 1926 to unify the northern and southern
factions of the Nazi party.

In spite of missing his morning sleep, Ralph said that he had
'quite fallen in love with the town' and adds mysteriously that
'Bamberg will always be memorable to me for effecting a cure
which I should have looked on as a divine miracle had I been at

The Bauhaus in Dessau

Lourdes.' Was it perhaps the end of the persistent earache that Ralph had first experienced in New Zealand in 1927?

Throughout the tour, Ralph and Angus visited palaces, churches, art galleries and other sites such as Wagner's house ('interesting but hideous') with an earnestness of purpose lapsing into pomposity:

> In the middle is a fountain surmounted by an iron crown surrounded by candles. When the water is switched on this object slowly mounts on a column of water about 25–30 feet in the air. This was much admired by our fellow sightseers but was too much for our seriousness.

He often disapproved of fellow tourists: 'the streets of Oberammergau thronged with charabancs packed with Americans, their disgusting voices ringing everywhere.' The whole experience of the Passion Play at Oberammergau was a disappointment. They had 'good seats in the 27th row' but it rained, and 'the cruxifixion [*sic*] was produced in the most horrifyingly realistic manner and was almost unnecessarily distressing'. They attended several operas at Bayreuth and motored out to rural villages: 'There was a dance going on with the local boys and girls. It was amusing to watch,' says Ralph the onlooker, not the participant.

At points in the journey Ralph and Angus met up with friends from England, including Charlotte Bonham-Carter. As with all travel, there were difficulties along the way—inclement weather, theatre tickets that had not been booked, a 'smelly, bad hotel', and in Munich he experienced something that occasionally confronts travellers: 'I should not like to say what is going on in the next room while I am lying in bed, writing up these last two days.'

For the final two weeks of their stay in Germany, Ralph and Angus were accompanied by two sisters, Ina and Elizabeth, the daughters of a German major. It is only when they part company that Ralph mentions them in his diary:

> I have enjoyed being with them on the whole very much, and for Elizabeth I have nothing but praise—she is amusing, intelligent and very easy. Ina is far more egotistical and exacting [...] she has certainly never said a word of thanks for me conveying her about Germany in my car [...]. However I must not be captious as we have had a very amusing fifteen days and I have seldom laughed more.

Travelling on through a rainy Salzburg, Berchtesgaden, Innsbruck, Lucerne, Berne and Grenoble, they arrived at the end of August at Grasse where 'the atmosphere seemed to change. The sky was blue and the air was warm [...]. Reached Arthur Payne's at 6:30 and Alan Pryce-Jones there as well.' Pryce-Jones, another old Etonian and Oxford alumnus, was later to become editor of the *Times Literary Supplement* and a Liberal MP. On arrival Ralph made a quick change into 'a St Tropez shirt and flannel trousers', and then they were whisked off to dine 'with a Mrs Sholto Douglas, an astonishing woman who had collected an equally astonishing collection of guests. Everyone rather tipsy and not very amusing.'

Ralph and Angus soon settled into Riviera life: 'We had an enchanting fortnight with Arthur. I feared at first that it was going to be too social for us', but they had days lounging by the pool chatting with fellow guest David Horner, the lifelong partner of Osbert Sitwell. The Antibes coast was 'a pandemonium of human flesh' but Ralph found a quiet corner: 'at a secluded spot facing the open sea […] I sunbathed without reserve and eventually got burnt from head to foot without the customary polite interval.'

The pair turned their bronzed faces homeward at the end of September, stopping in Paris to dine with Victor Cunard at Prunier's. Cunard was a diplomat who had been a lover of the diarist Harold Nicolson (whose biographer was to be James Lees-Milne) and who later became *The Times* correspondent in Venice, where Ralph was frequently to see him in later years. Then onwards to Brussels passing through the distressing 'war area with few trees and hideous villages', Antwerp for the World Fair, Amsterdam for the Rijksmuseum and finally Haarlem to see the Frans Hals Museum. The indefatigable travellers disembarked at Harwich on 3 October and Angus took his train to York while Ralph motored to London and then to Hinton, meticulously recording that: 'My speedometer stood at 22,300 miles when I reached London, a trip of nearly 3,000 miles in 3 months.'

A further lengthy trip—longer than expected, due to an extraordinary turn of events—followed in 1931, this one to France and Italy. Ralph left the country well before the start of the tourist season, on 31 January, and another example of his shyness is recorded in his diary: 'Left Victoria at 11 on the Golden Arrow. Not a soul on the train I knew by sight, thank God, except Lloyd George!'

In Paris he was met by George Bambridge, a diplomat some-what older than Ralph, who was married to Rudyard Kipling's daughter Elsie. The couple bought Wimpole Hall near Cam-bridge in 1937 and bequeathed it to the National Trust in 1976, when Elsie died, childless. Ralph was always interested in motor cars and records that George had two cars, one a new Voisin, the other a Minerva, and both exceedingly luxurious.

Ralph spent a couple of days in Paris, drinking cocktails, eating at fashionable spots like La Pelouse and Le Bœuf sur le Toit and bumping into Sacheverell Sitwell and Raymond Mortimer at a party. But it was not all frivolity; he also studied architecture and interiors, with visits to Versailles and a series of Parisian hôtels.

Travelling on to Toulon by sleeper, Ralph was met off the train by Hugh Cholmondeley and his companion Carlo, and they ac-companied him by boat to Naples: 'Thank God there is nobody we know on board, except Jim Sherborne who I expected to see. I noticed [Jim] regarding Carlo's plus fours and beret with some surprise.' Jim Sherborne (1873–1949) was Ralph's uncle, the 6th Baron Sherborne, and the man who had sold Zoffany's conversa-tion piece *The Dutton Family* in 1929.

On arrival in Naples, Ralph met Paul Wallraf, 'a member of the Cologne family that established the Wallraf-Richartz Muse-um [...] and a collector of old master drawings who had homes in London and Venice'. Wallraf was to become a close friend of Ralph, and a rival collector, but Ralph feared that 'he and Carlo may not hit it off'. The weather was so bad in Naples that the party decided to move on with 'our 9 or 10 expensive pieces of luggage—crockodile [*sic*] pigskin and so forth' to Sicily where they found the hotels uncomfortable, expensive and flea-ridden. In Taormina there were 'too many of our compatriots in dinner jackets'. Moreover there 'was a huge wedding going on [...] not my sort of fun'.

'Uncle Jim', James Huntly Dutton, 6th Baron Sherborne

After a fortnight Paul Wallraf left to return to Hamburg, and Ralph travelled to Syracuse for lunch with David Horner, whom he had met the previous year in France, and his partner Osbert Sitwell. Osbert would go on to organise an exhibition with Ralph's decorator Ronald Fleming a year later in 1932, though exactly who introduced who to whom is unclear. This appears to be the first meeting between Ralph and Osbert; they were to become close and enduring friends. Ralph spent a happy afternoon with Osbert discussing their pedigrees and 'comparing our trees', and he concluded that once past Osbert's 'slightly alarming manner he is very entertaining'. Next day, Ralph lunched with some friends of Carlo, a couple called the Count and Countess of Wachtmeister. The count—a large man, an accomplished musician and composer, and also an adventurous traveller—was Swedish and his wife was American. Wachtmeister was a genuine aristocrat and diplomat, but Ralph was not impressed because the man was, according to Ralph's diary, 'so sodden with drink as to be almost beyond speech'.

At this point in the diary there is a gap of six days, and then, on 15 March, Ralph records in retrospect the beginning of a nightmarish few weeks. It began with the arrest of Hugh and Carlo and the detainment of the Wachmeisters, in the belief that they were a gang of international jewel thieves. The police were also suspicious of Ralph; they searched his rooms and questioned him, but never arrested him. In fact, Ralph comes out of this incident well, acting as a constant support for his friends, contacting the British Embassy, getting the Duca di Bronte (a descendant of Nelson who had an estate on the slopes of Mount Etna) to write to the Italian authorities, seeking advice from Sir George Sitwell, who travelled down from his castle at Montegufoni, and probably paying for solicitors, medical help and food for the prisoners. He also wrote to several MPs in the hope that they would raise the matter in Parliament, and Bob Boothby (part of the Uffizi Society set) spoke to the Foreign Secretary. His intervention was widely covered in British newspapers, and was even reported in the *Singapore Free Press* under the headline 'Imprisoned Without Trial', with Boothby quoted as saying: 'There is no foundation for the suspicion that Mr Cholmondeley had anything to do with the theft. Anybody who knows him knows that such a charge is absurd.'

It must have been a dreadful experience for Ralph. Hugh became very ill in prison, and there were several expectations of release that were dashed at the last minute: 'I think today was the most disheartening day we have had since this nightmare started,' Ralph records. When Hugh's parents rushed to their son's aid, it was Ralph who met them and looked after them.

After seventeen days in gaol, Hugh was released but Carlo remained locked up and the saga rumbled on. It was not until 30 May that everyone was declared innocent by a presiding judge who instantly threw the case out after hearing the weakness of the 'evidence'. It had all been a great misunderstanding. There had indeed been a jewel theft at the hotel, but in some mix-up with luggage Hugh and Carlo had wrongly been put in the frame. The police thought it only natural that they should have suspected such an oddly assorted cosmopolitan party; they did not apologise. Ralph and the rest of the party quickly headed for home.

Sometime in 1933 Ralph became a governor of a local school in Hampshire—probably the school in the village of Kilmeston adjacent to the Hinton estate—a position he held for fifty years until the school closed in 1983. It was the first of many local and, later, national appointments to public bodies.

In August of 1933 Ralph once again travelled with Angus Holden, this time to France and Spain.

They had been working together on a guidebook called *English Country Houses Open to the Public,* which was published by Allen & Unwin in 1934. This trip to France was undertaken in order to research their next co-authored work for the same publisher, *French Châteaux Open to the Public,* which came out in 1936. Unsurprisingly, a car features in the diary: they were travelling in a very grand Delage.

Unfortunately it broke down and they took it to the Delage factory in Paris where they were told: '*Votre voiture est morte*', which Ralph describes as 'a most distressing piece of information'.

With an expensive new engine, they continued on their way through France and over the Pyrenees, travelling south as far as Torremolinos, 'this tiny village,' from where Ralph wanted to send a telegram home but was told: 'Impossible. This is a Post Office.'

Ralph and Angus did not enjoy Spain: 'It is surprising to find a country in which the food is worse than in England.' In spite of finding 'their physical beauty a pleasure', Ralph's reaction to the Spaniards is frankly racist: 'one admires their ability to sleep

1933 Delage D8S Coupé

for hours in any position however uncomfortable [...] one would think that the task of welding this lethargic people into an efficient nation must be beyond the power of any government. Attempts as yet have done little but stir up that latent brutality which lurks deep in the heart of the Spaniard.'

After taking in Córdoba and Toledo, Angus decided to return to Yorkshire from Madrid ('a political crisis is going on here') because his father was ill, while Ralph drove home via Biarritz and Paris. The trip had lasted for two months and the odometer recorded a total of 3,500 miles.

Ralph was becoming ever more keen to start work on realising his dreams at Hinton. He did not dare interfere with the house, but in 1934 he persuaded his father, who agreed 'with some reluctance', to make alterations in the garden by adding a sunken garden with formal beds and a wide grass path below the balustrade of the upper terrace. Ralph paid for this himself, from a lucky profit of £200 on the stock exchange.

Later in the year Angus and Ralph were off again, first by air fleetingly to Paris (the Ritz bar and dinner at Le Doyen), then on to Toulon to be met on the platform by Hugh and Carlo. On 25 August 1934 Ralph wrote in his diary: 'I am 36 today. The day seems to have passed in an orgy of champagne.' The trip continued to Venice, and then by boat and train through Dalmatia calling at Split, Trogir, Sarajevo, Zadar and Montenegro to see churches and palaces, Roman ruins and medieval forts. On the return journey, Angus returned home from Paris, but Ralph 'hired a Citroën at great cost' and was joined by a friend named John. Together they toured the cathedrals and châteaux of northern France for a further three weeks.

Back at Hinton in early October, Ralph's father was deteriorating. He died on New Year's Day 1935, a fortnight short of his eighty-eighth birthday. It is clear from Ralph's comments in a letter to his friend Charlotte Bonham-Carter that his father's final years had been a worrisome burden, both to him and to his mother:

11/1/1935

My Dear Charlotte,

Thank you so much for your letter and sympathy. The events are terribly distressing even when one has contemplated them for years, as we have had to. It makes a great break in all our lives […]. My poor mother was very shattered but I hope will soon be better now that the worry of years is over.

It is also clear from the same letter that not only Ralph, but the entire family had been thinking about what to do next:

I have no notion as yet how I stand but I very much hope it may be possible for me to make a few alterations here and then live in a more modest manner. I certainly have every intention of living here if it is possible […]. Luckily [my mother] is quite excited about the prospect of living at the

Bramdean Manor—Blanche and Ursula have set their hearts on converting the pair of derelict cottages at Joan's Acre about a mile from this house, and this scheme has my full blessing if it turns out to be possible. What Joane will do I am not sure, perhaps stay with my mother for a bit. I am still inundated with condolences and arranging endless details but when I can get up to London I should love to come and see you […].

Yours ever,
Ralph

In the event Ralph did not wait to find out 'how he stood' before embarking on the transformation of Hinton Ampner. The assessment of death duties took years, and the process was prolonged by his father's solicitor proving to be not merely dilatory but fraudulent, eventually being sentenced to seven years in prison after having made away with large sums of his clients' money.

In addition to the Hinton Ampner estate, Ralph inherited several other properties from his father, including Bramdean Manor, Bedhampton Manor, Hartley Mauditt House, Pullens Farm, the Manor Farm at West Worldham, and Wick Hill Farm. He also inherited effects worth £197,000, equivalent to almost £10 million today. On top of that he had his own property in London, investments in stocks and shares resulting from his father's gift when he left Oxford and an income from being a Lloyd's 'name'.

Ralph was also earning money. He had been writing a book, *The English Country House*, that was to become something of a success. It was released by Batsford in November 1935, and he spent the £100 publisher's advance on a table with a blue-john top that had once belonged to Lord Curzon. This might well have been the best investment he ever made.

In his foreword to *The English Country House*, Osbert Sitwell makes this percipient observation about Ralph:

great as is his learning […] he never treats country houses purely as objects, dead things left behind by previous generations, but he makes them the exquisite and appropriate shells of various manners, various methods of living: this infuses the house of which he is discoursing with a new charm […] our author talks of his subject, English houses, with affection, as if visiting these halls, examining their furniture and associations were […] one of the joys of his life.

Which indeed it was.

The English Country House was well received. James Lees-Milne gave it to all his friends as a Christmas present in 1935 (Ralph's old companion from the Uffizi Society, Anthony Eden, got another kind of Christmas present that year—he became Foreign Secretary). The book had a long life, running to many editions and appearing as a paperback in 1962. In 2022 *The Times* printed an obituary of the architect Nicholas Johnston (whose clients included Paul Getty and Mick Jagger) noting that Johnston, who was confined in bed by illness as a child, had been inspired to become an architect after he 'spent hours staring at corniced ceilings and drawing buildings, influenced by a 1935 book, *The English Country House* by Ralph Dutton'.

By the end of 1935 Ralph was a successful author, a well-travelled and well-read man with a sophisticated life in London and a group of close friends who shared his interests and enthusiasms.

It had been a pivotal year. He was now the head of his family and the owner of the Hinton Ampner estate and several other properties, which brought with them both riches and responsibilities—not least, his mother, three sisters and the sixteen staff who were employed at Hinton. At last he had a purpose in life and a free hand to do what he liked. He contemplated the task of transforming Hinton with relish.

Chapter Five:
1936–1939

Within eighteen months of his father's death, Ralph's life was transformed. In London he moved out of the flat in Piccadilly and into a terraced house at 21 Chapel Street, which runs between Belgrave Square (where his mother had mastered the art of driving a car) and Grosvenor Place (which marks the boundary of Buckingham Palace's garden). With the help of Ronald Fleming, he created there the very model of fashionable 1930s Vogue Regency, showing 'a precocious taste for neo-Classicism and especially brass-mounted Regency furniture, porphyry urns and lapis lazuli obelisks', in an attempt 'to find a style adapted for "English" living that was avowedly modern in spirit'. The approach was typical of Ralph, looking backwards in terms of form and inspiration, but forwards when it came to practicality and comfort. Despite Ralph's general reticence, he was happy, and perhaps proud, to have the interior featured in the press in February 1939. Another possibility is that he was doing Fleming a favour by publicising the work of his firm, Kelso Ltd.

Fleming took the view that there should be a close working partnership between himself and his clients:

> Rooms express the character of their owners to the last note. Rooms need to be lived in and loved by their owners to bring out their best qualities. The ideal client is someone of refined and imaginative taste, who can afford to work with his or her decorator as a helpful friend, and whose expert advice he or she is willing to take.

The interior of Dutton's home in Chapel Street, Belgravia, in 1939

In Ralph he had the perfect client, since Ralph was knowledgeable and wealthy enough to meet Fleming's criteria, but also modest enough to take advice, especially at this early stage in his development as a collector. They were to remain friends and collaborators for the whole of Fleming's life and, as we will see, Fleming played a major role in the decoration of Hinton.

While Chapel Street was being completed in 1936, work was just starting at Hinton. Ralph had immediately set to work in pursuit of his dreams, but the realisation of his ambitions was to take some time. Despite cautious counsel from some of those around him, he was 'fortunately [...] young enough to take no notice of sensible advice'. In the space of eighteen months, his mother and sisters had moved out of Hinton, he had decamped to another of his properties, Bedhampton Manor near Havant, and by July 1936 'the forecourt was filled with the contractor's tackle and impedimenta'.

Since his father's death, Ralph had appointed his friend Lord Gerald Wellesley, working in partnership with Trenwith Wills, as architects for the project. Gerry Wellesley, who unexpectedly became the 7th Duke of Wellington when his nephew was killed in action in 1943, was older than Ralph, having been born in 1885, but they shared many interests, including a fondness for both eighteenth-century architecture and hard stone furniture and ornaments. As collectors and decorators, they became simultaneously rivals and collaborators, but at this stage in the creation of Hinton, Wellesley was an important mentor and guide to Ralph, providing advice, sourcing materials and using his expertise to create formal architectural schemes and plans.

Like Dutton, Wellesley was a Hampshire man. When Wellesley succeeded to the dukedom, he also inherited Stratfield Saye, a house and estate to the north of Basingstoke, and both he and Ralph served their county in administrative posts, with Wellesley appointed Lord Lieutenant of the county from 1949 to 1960.

Wellesley's character was complex, and Chips Channon, who employed him (again working with Trenwith Wills) as architect and decorator for both his London and country houses, seems never to have quite made up his mind about him. In 1925 he described Wellesley as a 'cold, formal, unimaginative, brilliant creature', while in 1935 his diary records:

> A long day. Gerry Wellesley met us to decide colours for the library. He was rude and sulked like a small child. He is an extraordinary character, common yet distinguished; acutely obsessed with his Wellington origin yet democratic in some ways; he is pompous, stilted, witty yet humourless. In fact a ridiculous person altogether, for whom I have always great affection.

According to Evelyn Waugh, Wellesley was so proud of his

Gerald Wellesley, 7th Duke of Wellington

ancestry that he 'used to travel with a bust of his great ancestor'. According to Alan Pryce-Jones, his manner earned him the sobriquet 'The Iron Duchess'.

The writer and biographer Michael Bloch tells us that

> the phenomenon of male homosexuals marrying lesbians was not uncommon in the establishment world of the first half of the twentieth century. Such unions provided both parties with socially necessary camouflage; and where affection, common interests and mutual respect existed they could be surprisingly successful.

Bloch mentions Wellesley's 1914 marriage to Dorothy Ashton as an example, although they in fact separated (Ashton was descended from a wealthy cotton manufacturer, and she worked as an editor at the Hogarth Press, which is probably how she met Vita Sackville-West, who became her lover in 1922). Bloch provides other examples of such marriages, most of whom were friends of Ralph, including James Lees-Milne and Alvilde Chaplin and Michael Duff and Caroline Paget.

Wellesley was an excellent architect and played a prominent role in promoting art and design. The architectural historian John Cornforth has this to say of him:

> By nature a scholar and possessing a finely tuned, fastidi-
> ous taste, he became involved in many projects relating to
> the improvement of the arts of design, public taste and later
> preservation, particularly of country houses, and through his
> friendships and his houses he had an influence on a consid-
> erable number of people.

One of those people was Ralph Dutton.

Together, Dutton, Wellesley and Wills agreed a plan for Hinton: to demolish the old Victorian house (though not the servants'
wing), retain the Georgian core and build a new neo-Georgian
block around it. As the architectural historian John Martin Robinson puts it, the new build would have 'sashes and a parapet rather
than mullions and gables'. The old house was short of bathrooms;
the new one would have seven bedrooms and six bathrooms. The
old one was too big, with too many small rooms; the new one
would consolidate, simplify and be more commodious. Above all,
in place of the Victorian 'monstrosity', there would be something
beautiful: 'I could hardly believe I was to live in a house I could
look at without pain.'

All of this caused Ralph some psychological guilt:

> For a number of years after the transformation had taken
> place I would have a dream, it amounted I think to a night-
> mare, that my father had somehow come to life again and

The neo-Georgian reincarnation of Hinton Ampner, 1936

that I was under the necessity of explaining to him what had occurred.

The constructions at Hinton bucked the trend of the 1930s because many houses were being demolished, but not many were being built: 'the slump left few people in England with the confidence to build.' This worked to Ralph's advantage because he was able to purchase, and then incorporate into Hinton, interior features and furnishings of astonishing quality from magnificent eighteenth-century buildings that had been broken up earlier in the century. Today, it would be simply impossible to source such a rich array of treasures, regardless of the funds available to do so.

In a handwritten note on Foreign Office stationery—so probably written during the Second World War—Ralph made a list of architectural and decorative items that he had bought for Hinton, with notes on where they had come from. They included a mantlepiece for the hall from Hamilton Palace in Scotland;

28 . MAY 1937.

BEDHAMPTON MANOR, HAVANT.
HAVANT 424.

*Christopher Hussey records a visit to Ralph Dutton at Bedhampton Manor,
while Hinton was being rebuilt, 28 May 1937*

window linings, doors, a mantlepiece and grate from the Adelphi
in London; a ceiling from Lord Rosebery's house in Berkeley
Square; a mantlepiece from Clumber Park in Nottinghamshire;
and floorboards from Norfolk House in St James's Square. In
addition to fixtures, there were curtains from Lionel Rothschild's
house at 149 Piccadilly and from the Grange, a property eight
miles from Hinton that belonged to the Baring family of bankers.
Ralph also sourced fittings from architectural salvage merchants
and was delighted when Gerry Wellesley found a rare porphyry
chimney-piece for him in Staines.

One major difficulty Ralph faced when building began was
finding accommodation for the workforce, who had to live on site
since they had no daily transport of their own. Another problem

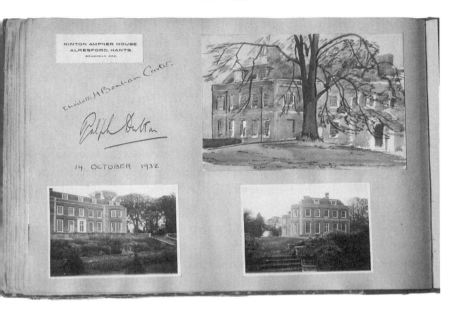

Christopher Hussey and Charlotte Bonham-Carter at Hinton Ampner,
19 October 1938

was the antagonistic relationship that developed between the clerk of works, who was acting as Ralph's man on the ground, and the contractor's foreman, who was in charge of actually doing the work. But things moved forward, as Ralph explained:

> Thus the work proceeded through the months, the straightforward lines of the neo-Georgian building gradually emerging through the Victorian Tudor as crockets, gables and battlements gave way to a brick parapet, and the plate glass and heavy stone mouldings of the windows were replaced by small paned sashes and wooden astragals.

Ralph and his close friends admired the spirit of the eighteenth century as well as its architecture and design. It was an idea that was to become attractive to others and in the mid-1930s the pace of interest in the period quickened. Christopher Hussey, who later wrote a definitive three-volume guide to the architecture of the Georgian period, together with Gerry Wellesley, the Sitwell brothers and Angus Holden were all approached to lend their names when the Georgian Group was founded in 1937 with the aim of protecting Georgian buildings. The Society for the Protection of Ancient Buildings was indifferent to the fate of anything built later than 1714, and public and official attitudes were no different. Ralph's friends, and Ralph himself, were gradually to change all that.

The work at Hinton did not prevent Ralph from continuing with his travels. In 1936 he spent three weeks in Bordeaux and the Dordogne. Travelling from Hinton 'with John in the Buick', they boarded a ferry at Newhaven, onto which a chauffeur had already loaded 'the Ford'. One highlight of this trip was lunch in Bordeaux with the Calvet family of wine shippers. The food was accompanied by 1900 Château Latour and 1874 Château Margaux. Ralph visited several famous vineyards in the area, including Cheval Blanc, Pape Clément and Haut-Brion. At the latter he 'determined to get Mr Berry to get me some of the 1934'. It is likely that this 'Mr Berry' was Charles Walter Berry, one of the family that ran Berry Bros & Rudd in St James's Street (where the firm continues to operate as it has done since 1698) and who was a close friend and business associate of the Calvet family. Charles Berry had probably provided Ralph with an introduction to the Calvets. It appears that the '34 Haut-Brion was delivered, because three years later Ralph's bank-book records a hefty payment to Berry Bros. & Rudd.

On Sunday 5 July 1936, Ralph made his first radio broadcast. Ralph's subject was the same as his recently published book, 'The Country House', and it was mentioned in the *Radio Times*:

This evening Ralph Dutton is to describe life in a country gentleman's house 250 years ago. A house set near the village, a formal garden, a mysterious grotto in a formal grove of trees; and in the house itself imposing rooms, Gobelin tapestry and marquetry furniture (both just coming in), magnificent beds, sumptuous meals. Yet one learns that the retinue of male servants who paraded by day in resplendent liveries were herded together in a cellar at night. Bathrooms were very rare, and slops were emptied out of the window.

Although building work at Hinton was progressing slowly, Ralph was already planning the interior decoration of the house. Gerry Wellesley provided a detailed plan for the library, and Ralph worked with Ronald Fleming on colour schemes. Acting sometimes alone, and sometimes with the guidance of Wellesley or Fleming, Ralph was also acquiring furniture, paintings, objects and textiles for the interiors. All of this involved considerable expense, and at the start of 1937 Ralph sold some of his investments in shares in order to fund the purchase of further fixtures, fittings and decorations.

In March of that year, Ralph received a letter from a Hampshire neighbour who was to become a close and lifelong friend:

My Dear Ralphy

Please forgive typewritten letter but my secretary has not had a great deal of work to do today so I thought it would be a good plan to give her some practice. Am sending you a photograph of myself duly autographed etc. which no doubt one day you will be able to sell for a large sum of money, and with any luck pay off a mortgage on the Towers. My secretary however does not agree with this view […].

With much love my dear Ralphy,

from Augustus.

Augustus Agar, VC, brightens a dull day in 1937

Augustus Agar is described in *The Dictionary of National Biography* as 'the epitome of the "sea-dog" of British Naval tradition: honourable, extremely brave and totally dedicated to King, country and the Royal Navy.' The naval historian Alfred Draper, in his book *Operation Fish*, says that he was a 'slim, impeccably uniformed man with an extremely courteous manner'.

Agar led an extraordinary life. He was born in Ceylon in 1890, the thirteenth child of an Irish tea-planter. His mother died shortly after his birth and he was sent to England at the age of eight. Four years later his father died, and he was then brought up by an older brother. At fourteen he entered a naval academy and was at sea from then on, serving in many ships and earning many honours, including the Distinguished Service Order (DSO) and the Victoria Cross (VC)—the latter is on display at the Imperial War Museum. Agar's first wife was Mary Petre—they married in 1920 and were divorced in 1931—so it is possible that Ralph met the Agars through his Berlin friend Francis Petre. Augustus married again, to a woman named Ina, and the couple, who lived nearby in Alton—in fact they settled in Hartley Mauditt where Ralph's father had owned the estate before the First World War—appear frequently in the Hinton visitors' book throughout the succeeding decades. Ralph remembered Ina in his will, leaving her £500.

In addition to overseeing changes at Hinton and making frequent visits to Europe, Ralph was continuing to write. Batsford published *The English Garden* in 1937, as a logical follow-up to *The English Country House*. Always modest, Ralph claimed to be 'not a very knowledgeable plantsman', but the book shows that he did at least know a great deal about garden history.

Ralph's interest in Hinton's garden had been growing for a decade. The first planting he undertook was of trees on the estate, a long-term project designed to enhance the views from the garden and the house, that shows a certain confidence in the future. In 1935, as we have seen, he created the sunken garden to improve the expansive southern view from the house.

He created a number of ha-has at the edge of the garden, consciously taking to heart the famous advice of Alexander Pope:

> Let not each beauty ev'rywhere be spied,
> Where half the skill is decently to hide.
> He gains all points, who pleasingly confounds,
> Surprises, varies, and conceals the bounds.

Throughout his life Ralph cherished the view at Hinton, and as and when opportunities arose he bought parcels of land in order to protect it. He loved the view so much that he created a small window at the correct height, in order to enjoy looking out over the park while seated on the lavatory in his bathroom. A well-placed ashtray adds to the comfort and convenience.

As the garden developed in the mid-1930s and beyond, Ralph experimented with plantings and layouts. Some innovations failed, such as the first attempt to create a garden in a hidden dell—he thought it would suit half-hardy plants but it turned out to be a frost pocket. He was keen to learn from other gardens and gardeners and went looking for ideas, particularly at Hidcote, an Arts and Crafts-inspired garden in the Cotswolds, and Sissinghurst (the garden created by Vita Sackville-West and Harold Nicolson), which he then adapted to his own purposes. For example, he created a formal structure containing various garden 'rooms', but unlike those at Sissinghurst and Hidcote, Ralph's are not confined spaces; his intention was 'to make the garden "flow" so that a visitor is led on from point to point, and vistas, long or short, come here and there into view'. Despite seeking inspiration from other places, as the garden historian Tim Richardson has noted,

> there is no single precedent for Hinton Ampner: it combines simplicity and modesty of tone with an uncompromising architectural attitude—Dutton was a historian who produced books on the English country house and garden in the 1930s. Brent Elliott has usefully compared Dutton's reductionist ideas with the stylishness that was one of the avowed aims of Modernism, quoting Dutton in *The English Garden* (1937): 'Only with the present century, so one likes to think, has that just alliance of interesting detail, coupled with broad and simple lines, untrammelled by particular style or fashion, been achieved'.

Ralph paid frequent visits, sometimes several times a year, to the Royal Horticultural Society at Wisley, to the Savill Gardens in Surrey, and to the Sir Harold Hillier Gardens near Romsey in Hampshire. During each visit he made notes of plants that he liked and would then order them, usually in bulk, and most often from Hillier's Nursery.

Nearing the age of seventy, Ralph looked back and understood what he had been trying to achieve: 'I have learnt during the past years what above all I want from a garden: this is tranquility.' He succeeded in his aim to such an extent that Hinton became famous mainly for its garden; indeed as at the date of writing (2023) a sign saying 'Hinton Ampner Garden' still advertises the property from the A272.

Chapter Six:
1939–1945

Progress on the house and garden continued slowly, and as war approached it became increasingly difficult to acquire building materials. Despite the house being incomplete, Ralph, in a state of some exasperation, was determined to move in, so he asked the contractors to concentrate their efforts on the service wing in order to have at least a part of the house habitable. He moved back to Hinton during the midsummer of 1938, and as the rooms of the main house were sequentially completed 'in the early summer [of 1939], and although the bare plaster walls were not very handsome', he 'was able to get [his] furniture out of store, put carpets down and curtains up, so that the house had a reasonable appearance'.

As soon as he moved in he was eager to entertain, and the first person he invited was Charlotte Bonham-Carter: 'will you come and stay for a quiet weekend on August 11th?' She was his first and last guest because Ralph's occupancy of Hinton was to be short-lived. On 29th August 1939 he received a telegram from the Office of Works, acting under the Emergency Powers (Defence) Act 1939, informing him that Portsmouth High School would be taking the house over in two days' time, when charabancs full of schoolgirls would arrive. This was a devastating blow: 'For me it was a moment of intense bitterness: just as the many months of work and effort had reached their culmination, all was snatched from me,' but with typical stoicism, Ralph commented that 'the situation had to be accepted, and picking up my suitcase, I left'.

Ralph's friend Osbert Sitwell wrote to commiserate:

My Dear Ralph,

I cannot tell you how disturbed and angry I was to hear from David of your lovely house being turned to so base a purpose. It really is too [underlined three times] maddening, and you have all my sympathy. I hope the war won't prevent me from seeing you soon.

In fact, many country house owners considered occupancy by a girls' school to be the height of good fortune. The Duke of Devonshire *invited* the girls of Penrhos College to decamp to Chatsworth during the war 'reasoning that "if the house is full of schoolgirls the authorities will not allow soldiers anywhere near the place"'. Ralph eventually came round to the same opinion: 'how fortunate I was to have my house populated by little girls, although they were hardly angels.'

In the decades after the war, the girls of Portsmouth High School held reunions at the house, and some wrote to Ralph about their experiences. One of them, referring to an old but widely known legend that there had been a ghost at Hinton, informed Ralph that 'I was a very small girl and experienced quite a number of genuine hauntings […]. I felt an overall atmosphere of evil and I was very frightened.' It would be hard not to take offence, but Ralph's good manners prevailed in his reply:

The impression you had here as a child of five certainly astonishes me, as no-one else has experienced anything of the sort. Indeed there is no reason why anyone should, as the haunted house was demolished 174 years ago, and the present building is not on the same site. The suggestion that there is a sinister feeling about the house seems to me to be very wide of the mark, for no place could have a more serene and cheerful atmosphere.

Portsmouth High School at wartime Hinton Ampner:
top left: girls in front of the house; top right: choral class;
bottom left: picnic with Miss Lindsay, August 1940;
bottom right: planting potatoes, c. 1940

Most of the other girls appear to have agreed with Ralph, and one 'lucky schoolgirl who stayed there during the war' later wrote in appreciation:

> We always thought what a kind man you must be to let the children have your house. I have wonderful memories of climbing along the parapet, which was a wonderful dare [...]. Many a girl sat crying for her parents behind the curtains on the window seat in the 'ballroom' [...] throughout the air-raids we sat each side of the service wing passage with our eiderdowns wrapped around us.

While the nation waited for something to happen during the period of the 'phoney war', the summer and autumn of 1939 were to be a busy time for Ralph. His next book, *The Land of France*, co-written with Angus Holden and with a foreword by Raymond Mortimer, was published by Batsford, and then, on 12 September 1939, only eleven days after the declaration of war, Ralph received a letter from the Foreign Office appointing him as a temporary clerk in the Communications Department, at a salary of £400 per annum. There he stayed 'for 69 months, neither rising nor falling in my status'. That status, however, was not as lowly as the title of 'clerk' suggests; being a clerk was a senior and respected position, involving considerable responsibilities.

When he arrived back at the Foreign Office, where he had worked in the First World War, his old companion from the Uffizi Society, Chips Channon, was already there, serving as Parliamentary Private Secretary to Rab Butler, who was himself a Parliamentary Under-Secretary of State. Both Butler and Channon had been pro-German appeasers, Channon especially so. Fifteen months later, in December 1940, another Uffizi member, Anthony Eden, was to become Foreign Secretary for the duration of the war. For some years Ralph held a passport bearing the message, 'His Brittanic Majesty's Principal Secretary of State for Foreign Affairs requests and requires [...]', that was signed by Anthony Eden, a man who had sat next to him for a photograph twenty years earlier.

Given the speed with which Ralph was re-recruited to the Foreign Office, it seems likely that he had been in touch with his old employer in anticipation of the outbreak of hostilities, which in turn suggests that he was more clear-eyed than some about Germany's aggressive intentions. He himself claims that 'concentrating on my own interests, I was taking, I fear, little notice of international affairs', but this seems disingenuous.

Ralph has left no evidence about his political views, but his patriotism can be in no doubt. In addition to working in the Foreign Office during the day, he spent the wartime nights as a fire-watcher. So did T. S. Eliot, who evokes the experience, in 'Little Gidding' from *Four Quartets*:

> The dove descending breaks the air
> With flame of incandescent terror [...].

The Fire Watchers Order, a government decree made in September 1940, made it compulsory for all commercial and public premises to have fire watchers on duty at all times, and they were trained to deal with small fires. Oral history accounts from the time contain examples of what it was like, such as Teddy Briggs's in East London:

> In 1940, at the age of 16, I was allowed to serve with the men as a 'Fire Watcher'. This entailed spells of duty on the roof of buildings to smother any incendiary bomb in our section with sandbags or, if a fire had already started, to drench it with water using a stirrup pump and a bucket of water until the fire brigade took over. The Luftwaffe followed this fire raising exercise by dropping HE [high explosive] bombs that caused the fires to spread even more. There were many fatalities and casualties amongst the ordinary civilians as well as the Police, Fire and Ambulance services who were taking the injured to over-worked hospitals.

In January 1940 Ralph was formally assessed for active service, but at his medical examination was judged, in the emphatically clear words of the military, 'Grade III THREE (Vision)', which meant that, as in the First World War, he was unable to join any of the services on account of his poor eyesight. The report also notes that his eyes are hazel, his height 6 feet and his hair at this point grey/black.

At the age of forty-one, pushed out of his own home only a few months after having moved into it, Ralph found himself living in his house in Chapel Street in London, which at least was within easy walking distance of his office. As Ralph says: 'The break with my former life was sudden and complete. It resembled having a plaster pulled sharply off one's stomach, the pain was intense but not prolonged.' The Foreign Office allowed him two days off in sixteen, and he spent most of those visiting his mother in Bramdean and his sister Joane who had settled as a dairy farmer in the area. He was therefore able to keep a close eye on Hinton, and one of the Portsmouth girls later wrote to him to say that she had seen him on one of those visits: 'I am conscious of a debt of gratitude to you for the time I spent at Hinton and I do wish that our presence there had not made you so unhappy.'

Despite the war, Ralph's determination to complete Hinton never wavered. In the summer of 1940, he heard that an Adam ceiling from 37 Berkeley Square, with roundels painted by Angelica Kauffman, which he had purchased in 1939 at the suggestion of Gerry Wellesley, would have to be installed at Hinton or it would be destroyed as it could no longer be kept in storage. Amazingly he managed to find workmen to put up the ceiling in the dining room during the school holidays.

Ralph left no record of what he did during the war, and the National Archives give no clue about his activities as a civil servant. His greatest skill lay in his command of French, and since he was recruited into the Communications Department, he probably therefore worked as a translator and possibly as a liaison point. It is known that he travelled to Belgium and France on Foreign Office business at the end of the war, suggesting that he was in touch with both the Belgian and French governments-in-exile during the hostilities. If that is the case, then Ralph had a difficult job that required great diplomatic skills (which he possessed), given that relations between Winston Churchill and General de Gaulle were so strained. Their relationship has been described by Simon Berthon, author of *Allies at War*, as 'a roller coaster of mutual admiration, suspicion and, on Churchill's part, loathing'.

It is also possible that Ralph travelled to the Irish Republic in 1942 or 1943. When Ralph published *A Hampshire Manor* in 1968, he received an intriguing letter from William Mandeville Anderson of White Lodge, Dublin:

> Dear Ralph
>
> Having said this I only hope I am writing to the right person. [From reading your book I think] you must be the Ralph Dutton posted to the British Embassy in Dublin during the war. Perhaps you do not even remember me but we used to have a few drinks together. I was so interested in your book, because to a very much lesser extent I have tried to emulate you, having purchased two old Regency houses [...] and tried to bring them to life. This being Dublin and me being a bachelor, the fact of me wanting two large houses has raised a few eyebrows, but never mind [...]

If Ralph was in Dublin at this time, he may have encountered some of his fellow-countrymen. John Betjeman and his wife were stationed there, with John very successfully acting as press attaché at the British Embassy; and Laurence Olivier was shooting the Agincourt battle scene for the film of *Henry V* with the help of hundreds of Irish extras.

Although the exact nature of Ralph's wartime activities is unclear, a letter that he wrote to his friend Charlotte Bonham-Carter shows his state of mind. It was written at the end of May 1944, at a point when the whole country must have been ground down and exhausted, and Ralph was no exception:

My dear Charlotte,

So very many thanks for your letter and photographs. Your life sounds most strenuous and I am not surprised you have no energy for any further activity. I find that after battling with work and colleagues all day or all night, to return home to peace and solitude is the greatest treat imaginable. But how one longs for a little living and gaiety! I hope we shan't be too old to enjoy life again when the war ends but if it continues much longer I personally feel all my resilience will have disappeared. I wonder how one will re-adjust to a lei-sured life, will one be miserably bored? Will one feel one ought to be working all day? At this hour of the night (it is 3 a.m.) even the end of the war seems to have a darker side […]. I go to Bramdean later today, and wonder how I shall find my poor fruit trees and shrubs at Hinton. When I was last there, before the frost, the garden was looking rather lovely in spite of untidiness but now with the vagaries of the weather and the return of the horrible children it will be rather dreary I expect. Ursula's [i.e. his sister's] house was burnt down a few weeks ago—a great misfortune when it is so difficult to rebuild.

Much love,

Ralph

Despite the war, local life in Hampshire continued and on the first working day of 1944 Ralph received a letter from the Privy Council Office appointing him Sheriff for the County of South-ampton (that is, Hampshire, which was called the County of Southampton for administrative purposes between 1889 and 1959). A sheriff's duties at that time were to help with Royal visits, to play a role in the constitutional and judicial functioning of the coun-ty, and generally to encourage voluntary groups and civil society.

Inevitably, the war brought with it a tightening of belts, and within the month the Privy Council followed up their first letter with another imposing new strictures: 'The Lords of the Council have had under consideration the expenses attaching to the Shrievalty and are of the opinion that further economies are desirable […]. The employment of footmen and trumpeters and the provision of banners should be dispensed with.' *Sic transit gloria mundi.*

The war was taking its toll but there was hope, and as Ralph writes: 'Slowly and monotonously the years passed and by the early spring of 1945 it was clear that the war in Europe was in its last phase.' Things were looking up. He was informed that the girls' school would be moving out after Easter and that he could return to Hinton: 'But alas, my joy was of the shortest.'

In the first week of April, a letter arrived informing Ralph that the Astronomer Royal would be visiting Hinton with a view to commandeering the house for a new observatory. Not surprisingly, Ralph was cast into utter despair. The Service Departments 'had complete autocratic power' and could simply slap a compulsory purchase order on Ralph's home. The officials arrived on 16 April and Ralph describes the scene:

> No host could have had more unwelcome guests, and no guests, as I could easily perceive, had less pleasure in seeing their host. They had not expected the owner to be present. I led the way into the house and made what was, I fear, a very emotional oration […]. The party looked acutely embarrassed, not for themselves but for me who was making an hysterical exhibition […] The Astronomer Royal, Sir Harold Spencer Jones, took me aside and spoke kindly to me but made it apparent that he was not deviating in any way from his nefarious project.

Ten days of sleepless nights followed, but then the cloud lifted as suddenly as it had appeared. Ralph was told that the committee had decided to locate the observatory at Herstmonceux Castle in Sussex instead of at Hinton.

Events were moving rapidly. Already buoyed by the letter from the Astronomer Royal, there was more good news, which Ralph records in a moving passage from *A Hampshire Manor*:

> [...] on 7th May the German government agreed to an unconditional surrender, and it was announced that 8th May was to be celebrated as V.E. Day. It happened to synchronise with my two days' leave from the Foreign Office, so I was able to organise a celebration at Hinton. Feverishly we built as large a bonfire as was possible at short notice on a high point of the ridge between the villages of Hinton and Bramdean, and from the local pub I was able to obtain a barrel of beer. As it grew dark a large concourse from the two villages assembled and at 10:30 precisely the barrel was broached and I set fire to the bonfire. It burned magnificently, the first flames of joy, as opposed to sorrow, that had lit the night sky for five and three-quarter years. From the ridge the dark landscape stretched away northward and southward into the invisible distance. The deep blue scene was suddenly broken by many little points of brilliant light where others all over the countryside were celebrating the joyful end of the long succession of sombre days.

Two weeks later, on 1 June Ralph was released from his employment at the Foreign Office with thanks and appreciation: 'I always had complete confidence in your judgement and I could always rely on any task entrusted to you being well done.' Two weeks after that Ralph's Registration Card records him formally moving from London to Hinton Ampner: 'I was at home again at last.'

Chapter Seven:
1945–1953

Ralph stood at his bedroom window in 1945, 'gazing out onto the chaos of what had once been a well-kept garden'. The terraces were covered with long grass and the ground underneath had been churned up by hundreds of schoolgirl feet running around during lesson breaks. The problem was not easy to fix because there was no machinery and, even if there had been, there was no petrol. As ever, a determined Ralph found a solution:

> I was lucky finding two elderly men expert in the use of the scythe. Thus during the long summer evenings they spent many hours rhythmically mowing the rough herbage—a Millet scene—till the terrace had once again some semblance of a lawn.

It was equally challenging to make progress with the house. Ralph found it deeply frustrating that the European countries he visited in 1946—France and Belgium—had ended rationing, whereas in Britain severe restrictions continued. Permits were needed to buy building materials and to get work done. The small sum of money that he had been paid to repair the property when Portsmouth High School departed could be used only for that specific purpose; the householder had no flexibility to use the money in any other way, not even to use it for decorating. Whenever Ralph applied to undertake work on Hinton, he was given permission to finish only one room at a time.

The first rooms that Ralph completed were the dining room and the library. These rooms 'aimed at the eighteenth century or Regency periods', with Ralph gradually replacing the heavy furniture that he had inherited with 'more attractive things'.

Ralph's decorating priorities gradually evolved. He came to consider the 'Vogue Regency' style to be correct for London, but not for the country. Instead he adopted an eighteenth-century look at Hinton, but one that avoided a strict historicist approach.

Ralph's design philosophy was not fully articulated, or indeed formed in the 1940s—in fact it was by creating Hinton that Ralph honed his sensibilities and tastes—but three decades later he wrote a foreword for the catalogue of the Hampshire Antique Dealers' Fair that sums up his thoughts in retrospect:

> In those houses where little change has taken place during the past two centuries one is accustomed to find English furniture set below landscapes and figure paintings of the Continental Schools, and a happy marriage they make in spite of their divergent origins. It is a marriage to which we have become so well used that we are apt to forget the useful lesson it provides for the collector: *that purity is not essential…* a room containing good quality furniture of many periods can have equal charm, and in addition if it represents the collection of one person, *will reflect strongly the personality of the owner.* Likewise old furniture can harmonise with modern pictures and is not at all out of place in modern rooms of good design. [Author's italics]

At Hinton Ralph pursued his personal enthusiasms for hard stone furniture and objects; eighteenth-, early nineteenth- and twentieth-century ceramics; seventeenth- and eighteenth-century paintings mainly of the Italian School; comfortable modern sofas; and idiosyncratic objects that he had collected along the way, such as a witty Directoire French thermometer noting cold and hot temperatures between *gelée* and *Sénégal.* The anchor for every room was the carpet—English, French or Irish—that set the tone and dictated the rest of the colour scheme. In everything from grand paintings to tea cups, Ralph bought only the highest quality.

Sir Brinsley Ford noted that, rather than collecting a particular artist or period, Ralph was interested in pictures that had decorative value in the house. This is not invariably the case but as a general rule it holds good. We also know from Ford's memoir that things, including rare treasures, were meant to be used and enjoyed at Hinton, not just looked at and admired: 'At Hinton the men were always given breakfast in their bedrooms. It would appear on a tray with a little Louis XV coffee-pot, and porcelain and linen that would have been acceptable to Madame de Pompadour.'

Ralph's personality is reflected strongly in his attachment to the orderliness and proportions of the eighteenth century and its exacting standards of craftsmanship, and also to the soothing complementarity of the colours that he deployed. His character can also be seen in the sentimentality of keeping an inherited hideous clock, his eccentric taste for jet jewellery, and in the nonchalance and style of drinking breakfast tea from Sèvres porcelain.

Despite the fact that the work at Hinton was unfinished and that Ralph was a very private man (he would have agreed with his decorator Ronald Fleming that 'more than ever today, the Englishman's home is his refuge and comfort from the bitter winds of a cruel world'), he was nevertheless happy to have his collections and rooms written about in *Country Life* and beyond. His Regency furniture was the subject of an article in the magazine

The drawing room windows looking south over the view
from Hinton Ampner

in December 1946. Its author, Margaret Jourdain, author of the 1934 book *Regency Furniture 1795–1820*, was the foremost expert on the subject. She sums up Ralph's collection as being 'the ideal of severity and simplicity'. Looking at Hinton today, or reading visitors' accounts of it in the 1950s, these are not the words that spring to mind.

In two successive weeks in February 1947, Ralph's friend Christopher Hussey wrote a main feature about Hinton in *Country Life*, in which he described the house's architectural history, Ralph's rebuilding work and the main internal features and decorative items. Hussey astutely noted that, for all Ralph's deprecation of the Victorian era, the house, 'notwithstanding its transformation to Georgian appearance', still had a flavour of the nineteenth century: 'It is as though charming and benign Victorian ghosts pervaded the latest edition of the house […].' To underline the point, a photograph of the drawing room is captioned: 'A room of the 1850s, virtually intact.' Ralph himself was happy with the room: 'it was light, gay and pretty, and I felt I had been right in retaining the nineteenth century detail when almost all else in the house aimed at the eighteenth century or Regency.' Then in July 1947, Ralph was mentioned yet again in *Country Life* in an article about Victorian conversation pieces.

A decade later, in September 1957, the magazine turned its attention to Hinton's garden. Lanning Roper, the garden designer who worked for Christopher Hussey at Scotney Castle, wrote: 'I always associate the words "restraint" and "elegance" with this fine formal garden.' In the same year the French magazine *Connaissance des Arts* published a lavishly photographed feature on Hinton under the headline '*Un Manoir de Goût Anglais*'.

By 1949 Ralph had still not been given approval to complete the drawing room and he ran out of patience. When a firm of builders offered him the opportunity to do the work without a permit, he took it. Many people in the area knew what was going on, because when the lights were switched on in the January dusk in an uncurtained room, it was clear to see. When questioned by neighbours he hummed and hawed, but he got away with it and never received a visit from the police.

The improvements at Hinton were not confined to the grand rooms, nor indeed to the house itself. Over the space of fifteen years following the war, things got better in the service wing and the estate cottages were also gradually refurbished, although progress was slow and in some cases non-existent. The writer Sarah Langford describes the state of one of the tenant farms when her grandfather took it over in 1959: 'The primitive kitchen has a well for water and a hole in its roof big enough to see the sky through.

The only heating comes from fireplaces. The lavatory is outside on scrubland [...].'

Mary Cross, who was housekeeper at Hinton from 1954 to 1986, recalled that in the immediate post-war period water was still drawn from a well, and that the cooking stoves at Hinton were run on smokeless anthracite, as were two boilers in the cellar that provided hot water and central heating.

In 1951 the Bramdean branch of the Women's Institute produced a history of the parishes of Bramdean and Hinton Ampner. In it they recorded that by that year electricity had been installed in the villages and was 'well-established, but water and public drainage have not yet arrived'. Mains water was introduced not long after, but many properties on the estate, including Hinton itself, still have their own drainage systems.

Mary Cross also said that the walled kitchen garden supplied almost all the vegetables and fruit that the house needed, including melons and peaches. Cream, milk, meat and game came from the farms and the estate, as did wood for the fires. The household was almost self-sufficient, with a few extras such as tea and coffee and cleaning materials being brought from Alresford and Winchester, and essentials like wine and spirits coming in from London. Country houses and estates like Hinton would form 'a living organism' according to the cultural historian Robert Hewison, and as such they 'preserved certain values of the past: hierarchy, a sturdy individualism on the part of the owner, privilege tempered by social duty, a deference and respect for social order on the part of those who service and support them. They reinforce those values in the present.'

As life settled into a routine after the war, Ralph developed a habit of spending Tuesday to Thursday or Friday in London and the weekends at Hinton. At some point in the 1950s or early 1960s, Ralph changed his London address, moving out of Chapel

Angus Holden and Ralph Dutton
in the garden at Hinton Ampner, c. 1950

Street and into a top-floor flat in Eaton Square. Every Monday morning he would let Mrs Cross know how many guests to expect the following weekend: 'occasionally he forgot and would telephone or send a postcard with his apologies.'

The weekends were planned with meticulous care. Ralph kept records of who was there and the food that was served, in order to make sure that the parties were convivial and that there was no repetition of the menu. He also hand-wrote each of the *placement* cards for the meals.

In his personal life Ralph had everything of the best. His shoes were made by John Lobb, his hats by Lock & Co. His stationery was ordered from Truslove & Hanson, his shaving soap came from Trumpers and his cigarettes from Sullivan & Powell. There was a Bentley in the garage. When his guests came for the weekend, they were treated to the same high standards of expensive simplicity. They could expect lunchtime sherry in front of the library fire, evening cocktails and first-rate claret with their meals. Their bathrooms were furnished with eau de Cologne and fresh cakes of Floris soap.

Weekend house parties at Hinton were relatively small, consisting of six or eight guests and occasionally twelve, though sometimes there would be only two or three. Everyone dressed for dinner. The numbers for Sunday lunch would usually be swollen by the addition of Hampshire neighbours such as Augustus Agar or Gerry Wellesley and their wives.

Most of the guests came from the conventional parts of the cultural world; many were old friends who Ralph had known since his schooldays or his twenties, some were fellow collectors and some were aristocrats, themselves owners of grand houses and estates.

In his book *The House Party*, Adrian Tinniswood describes weekends at Hinton:

> Safely reinstalled at Hinton Ampner, Ralph Dutton regularly held small parties for his select group of friends. Any weekend might see a gathering of figures at Hinton from the worlds of literature and the arts: Francis Watson, Director of the Wallace Collection, perhaps […] and the novelist L. P. Hartley, 'an extraordinarily cosy man to be with' according to a fellow guest; the biographer James Pope-Hennessy, who would stamp off into the garden to sulk if his fellow guests weren't sufficiently amusing; and Ronald Fleming, the society decorator who helped Ralph to create the interiors at Hinton. Ralph was a bachelor, and the redoubtable Christabel Aberconway, who in the years after the war lost both her husband and her lover, sometimes acted as hostess for him. Jane Abdy, wife of the art collector Sir Robert Abdy, brought her cats with her.

It is worth pausing to say more about some of these guests as their relationships with Ralph reveal some characteristics of the man himself.

James Pope-Hennessy was eighteen years younger than Ralph and had won the Hawthornden Prize for Literature in 1940 for his first book, *London Fabric*, at the age of twenty-two. Highly talented and sociable, he rose through the ranks in wartime, was recruited by military intelligence and then sent to Washington. He had a wide circle of friends, including writers such as James Lees-Milne, Raymond Mortimer and Harold Nicolson. After the war he became a noted biographer. However, Pope-Hennessy was hopeless with money; Lees-Milne takes up the story:

> Ralph greatly admired James's talent and came to the rescue
> [...] with gifts, not loans, of money. When he sensed that
> James was in financial straits he would pay large sums into
> his bank account without telling him. James would be pro-
> fuse with his thanks and write Ralph letters of heart-melting
> gratitude—that is to say , whenever he realised these bene-
> factions had been made. His bank manager did not hurry
> to impart the good news, which he feared might induce the
> benefacted to spend immediately on something he coveted
> in a book or antique shop.

Ralph, then, was a good friend in time of need. It may be that Ralph's generosity was prompted by an attraction to, or admiration of, Pope-Hennessy's dangerously daring private life. We have seen that Ralph was friends with several men who were entirely honest about their homosexuality, in spite of it being illegal. Pope-Hennessy fell into this category. He died in hospital in 1974, following a knife attack at his Ladbroke Grove flat. Lees-Milne commented: 'He was one of the most brilliant creatures I have known, but, alas, he was a bad friend.'

Francis Watson was at Hinton because of Ralph's connection with the Wallace Collection, where Watson was the director. Ralph had been invited to become a trustee of the Wallace by the Labour Prime Minister Clement Attlee in April 1948, when appointments to cultural institutions were free from party political interference, and he had accepted with alacrity. It was initially a seven-year appointment but as it turned out Ralph was to retain the position until 1969.

Ralph and Watson developed a close friendship because Ralph valued Watson's company as well as his learning and expertise, but Lees-Milne was notably less endeared:

> I never liked Francis Watson much, though he was good company. Always in good cheer, gossipy, mischievous, informative. Pleased with himself, very. Always the society man, but scratch the surface and there was a little bounder. One was pleased to see him, while dreading what he would say about one at the next party he attended. Undoubtedly very clever and an expert on French artefacts. Not Keeper of the Wallace Collection for nothing. Jane a rather dreadful woman, who revelled in the discomfiture of others. Why they married God alone knows; presumably both wished to keep up the pretence of being the marrying sort.

The art historian and collector Brinsley Ford has left a detailed memoir of his own first visit to Hinton on 1 January 1953, when he went to see Ralph's paintings with a view to including some in an exhibition being arranged by the Arts Council in honour of the new Queen's coronation. His notes provide insights into Ralph's character, as revealed by his surroundings and his conduct on the day. For example, Ford notes Ralph's attention to detail, his panache and his courtesy:

he had all the keys made in ormolu, their handles consisting of a stylised bunch of feathers—the Dutton crest […]. We went into luncheon in a beautiful room commanding a fine view. In this, as in every other room, the excellence of my host's taste was conspicuous. Apart from the Adam ceiling he had bought two large and elaborate sconces or *girandoles,* which fitted the spaces they decorated so well that they might have been made for them […]. The meal was as well appointed as the room. The table gleamed with highly polished silver and the food quite excellent. We started with some kind of fish soufflé, then pheasant with a wonderful variety of vegetables, then Xmas pudding and mince pies with brandy butter […]. Some first rate cheeses to choose from, and with it all some excellent burgundy. An elderly butler was in attendance. Our host […] has written books on France, on Architecture, and on the English Interior, and talks on these and other subjects in a scholarly way but without pedantry, and he has the flattering gift of appearing genuinely interested in the other person's opinions […]. The afternoon was spent going round the house which my host has made extremely comfortable […]. The afternoon ended with tea and Xmas cake after which my host drove me into Winchester to catch the train for London.

Ford was evidently seduced by Ralph's manner, his care and concern for his guest and the high standards achieved at Hinton; Ralph, he said, was 'delightful'. The feelings must have been reciprocated, because Ford and his wife became regular guests at Hinton's weekend parties. After the gruelling years of war and privation (rationing did not end until 1954, the year after Ford's first visit), an invitation to Hinton must have been a sybaritic treat.

Chapter Eight:
1953–1960

Throughout the late 1940s and 1950s Ralph kept up a steady stream of publications: *The English Interior 1500–1900* (1948), *Wessex* (1950), *The Age of Wren* and *English Country Houses* (both in 1951), *London Homes* (1952), *Normandy and Brittany* (1953), *The Victorian Home* (1954), *The Châteaux of France* (1957) and *English Country Houses in Colour* (1958). All of them were published by Batsford, who were delighted to have this prolific and popular author in their stable.

His working method was to produce handwritten pen-and-ink manuscripts which were then typed up by a variety of agencies in London and Winchester.

Ralph's books were respectfully reviewed in magazines and newspapers, from the *Oxford Mail* and the *Bolton Evening News* to the *Daily Telegraph* and the *Sunday Times*. *The Listener* commends Ralph's 'easy, urbane style'; the *Newcastle Evening Chronicle* found him to be 'informative without being ponderous' and *House and Garden* 'thoroughly recommends' his work.

It took Evelyn Waugh to prick the bubble. In December 1954 he reviewed Ralph's *The Victorian Home* for the *Sunday Times*. Under the heading 'Plush and Mahogany', he lays into the work saying it is:

> a book which cannot be wholeheartedly commended to any class of reader [...]. The illustrations are very poorly produced. The text is trite and patronizing [...] the only readers likely to derive enjoyment from it are those who indulge in

the badger-digging of literary blood-sports, the exposure of error.

In a letter dated 16 December 1954, Nancy Mitford wrote to Waugh:

> Darling Evelyn,
>
> How I shrieked at your review of that poor man's book. Ever since I can remember he has brought out some nice book every year & the reviewers have said so charming & people have given each other copies in the certitude of pleasing, & now all of a sudden a dreadful avalanche obliterates the poor fellow—for ever, I should think.

Waugh replied to her two days later:

> Dearest Nancy,
>
> [...] When I reviewed that Victorian book I took the writer to be a bumptious young puppy. I hear he is an aged and wealthy pansy. What astounds me is the standard of reviewing. The book was a congeries of platitude & misstatement like a prep-school examination paper on 'jellygraph'. I keep opening papers which say 'Mr Dutton's scholarly & penetrating work—impeccable taste—sumptuous production' etc.

Far from burying Ralph under an avalanche, the public continued to buy Ralph's books in numbers, and he continued to produce them. At this distance in time, it is possible to make a more clear-eyed assessment of Ralph as an author. In his favour, he wrote with a clarity and ease that was welcomed by the reading public. He wrote useful guides and popularised new areas of enquiry in interiors, architecture, gardens and foreign travel. His books were well illustrated and, for their time, reasonably well researched, given the lack of secondary sources and the difficulties of researching primary sources.

However, the academic R. C. Richardson points out some shortcomings:

> Dutton was never a dry-as-dust scholar whose own views on a topic were studiously kept out of sight. All the books he wrote are unashamedly subjective, judgmental, and down-to-earth. He knew what he liked and why, and told his readers so in a forthright manner [...]. Dutton's books tended to be short, 120 to 150 pages including illustrations was the norm [...]. None of the books had footnotes or guides to further reading. They all tended to finish abruptly without final stock-takings of the subject or any over-arching conclusions. There is no theorising, no philosophising. They do not probe deeply beneath the surface. They make no great demands on the reader. There are errors of detail.

In his 1950 book *Wessex*, Ralph is free with his opinions, as Richardson describes:

> Salisbury is 'the most beautiful county town in England'. The coastline from St Adhelm's Head to Portland Bill he accounted one of the loveliest in Britain. By contrast he found nothing positive to say about Trowbridge, the 'architectural horror' of Bournemouth, and the 'dull town of Gillingham'. Dutton's most poisonous venom however was reserved for Swindon, 'the Wigan of the South'.

As Ralph grew older, these characteristics became more pronounced. There are many letters in Ralph's archives from readers pointing out errors in his books, and he became more judgemental and dismissive as the years went by. In his last work, *Hampshire*, published in 1970, Basingstoke receives both barrels: 'Basingstoke, should one reach it, is a most unlovable town. It has never been remotely attractive, and at present is in the uncomfortable process of expanding from a population of 25,000 to one more than three times that size. It is definitely unpleasant.'

Yet despite, or perhaps because of, these failings, several of the books sold well. As we have seen, the most popular was one of his earliest from 1936, *The English Country House*, which ran to three hardback editions over fifteen years and then came out in paperback in 1962. The best written and most intimate is his book about Hinton Ampner, *A Hampshire Manor*, published in 1968, which has been reprinted as a National Trust Classic.

Evelyn Waugh, who collected Victorian paintings and had written about the Pre-Raphaelites, happened to review what was Ralph's most problematic book, *The Victorian Home*. As we have already seen, the Victorian era was an uncongenial period for Ralph. The book's subject was both huge and complex, and he struggled, becoming indecisive, muddled and prey to sweeping generalisations: 'the social order was changing, the way of life was slowly but distinctly altering, while taste was undergoing a radical transformation.' This is badly written history, both banal and unenlightening, but Ralph's own tastes are passionately and rather poetically revealed:

> We look back at the eighteenth century as at a panorama of all that was finest in the visual arts of this country. In architecture, in decoration, in painting, in the designing of furniture, in the moulding of landscapes; indeed in all that contributed to the pleasure and grace of living, the century seems to stand out as an era of consummate achievement. The whole of the hundred years seems bathed in golden sunlight, while the nineteenth century, like that part of the globe turned away from the sun, is overcast by a sombre grey shadow.

Having clearly stated his case, he then dithers, recognising that 'The violent alterations in taste which have taken place throughout history make it clear that standards are largely ephemeral.' There follows a convoluted passage where Ralph, at first sure of his own tastes and standards, comes to acknowledge that these things are not fixed and eternal but rather relative and shifting and depend on fashion and personal preference. In the end, Ralph leaves the reader confused and deflated.

By contrast, and unlike most of Ralph's books, *A Hampshire Manor* still reads as lively and engaging prose. On a limited canvas and with a subject that he knew intimately, he excelled.

In addition to writing books, Ralph was in demand as both a book reviewer and a writer of articles.

For example he wrote on 'The Future of Country Houses' for *The Times* and 'James Wyatt' for *The Times Literary Supplement*. He also became a public speaker and was asked to give lectures on the subjects he had written about. The year 1951 found him talking about 'Country Houses in the London Area' and 'English Domestic Architecture' in Southampton, and delivering a lecture on 'French Châteaux 1500–1800' to the Brighton Regency Society.

Ralph travelled frequently. His passports show him visiting France every year during the 1950s, with additional trips in some years to Spain, Italy and the Netherlands. The passports also show how his self-description and appearance change over the decades. In 1945 he is a civil servant with grey hair and hazel eyes, in 1955 an author, and from 1965 onwards, he becomes a white-haired landowner.

In the late 1940s and through the 1950s, Ralph increased the number and range of his commitments to public service. We have already seen that he had served in 1944 as the Sheriff of the County of Southampton, and had become a governor of the local primary school. He added another local role in 1954 as a trustee of the Hospital of St Cross, an almshouse for men founded in Winchester by Henry of Blois in the 1130s.

In addition to being appointed as a trustee of the Wallace Collection in 1948, in 1952 Ralph was invited to join the Executive Committee of the National Art Collection Fund, a position he held until 1972. The NACF (now called the Art Fund) was and is a charity that supports the purchase of paintings and objects by museums and galleries throughout the UK. The funds for these activities come from the organisation's membership, and the Art Fund has made a significant contribution to the nation's collections, being involved in the acquisition of more than 850,000 works since their founding in 1903. During Ralph's time, the fund was instrumental in helping the Tate Gallery to acquire Rodin's *Kiss* (1953), and the Walker Art Gallery to purchase Rubens' *Virgin and Child* (1960). The most important purchase, though, came in 1962, when the NACF organised a successful campaign to save the Leonardo Cartoon for the National Gallery.

In March 1955 Ralph's formal involvement with the National Trust began. He was invited to become a member of the National Trust's Historic Buildings Committee, the function of which was to advise on the suitability of properties for acceptance by the Trust and to oversee the condition of the Trust's properties. Christopher Hussey was already on this committee, and given their agreement about all things eighteenth century and their shared commitment to saving the nation's country houses, he and Ralph must often have been allies. In addition, the committee's chairman, Lord Chorley, was another devotee of the eighteenth century. James Lees-Milne held a part-time position as architectural adviser to the Trust, and was therefore also involved in this committee.

Ralph's connections with the Trust's activities expanded over the years as his expertise in many areas of the arts and in gardening were recognised. For example, together with Vita Sackville-West and Michael Rosse, he encouraged the Trust to set up a collection

Ralph Dutton (right) looking on as Francis Watson (left) shows
visitors round the Wallace Collection

of old shrub roses, which eventually resulted in the planting of the
rose garden in the walled garden of Mottisfont near Romsey, the
home of Ralph's Hampshire friend and frequent guest at Hinton,
Maud Russell.

The National Trust was one of a number of organisations, together with *Country Life*, the NACF and the various national
galleries and museums, where enthusiasts for architecture and
the arts met together, forming professional acquaintances and
friendships. As a group they had a huge influence on British culture. It was they who decided what would be purchased, shown
and valued; it was their tastes that influenced the national collections, and their books and scholarship that moulded public taste.

Patrician, usually well-connected by birth and education, male, often rich, they were a half-hidden but powerful group, who formed a self-selecting oligarchy. Sometimes they were employed in organisations (and sometimes without remuneration); they served on committees and boards; they wrote articles and books; they lent paintings and objects. As well as meeting each other when they sat on boards and committees, they gathered at weekend parties and in London clubs. They became known as the great and the good, and their tastes defined what was becoming known as 'heritage'.

James Lees-Milne's biographer Michael Bloch comments on this group:

> Jim had by this time [the 1950s] a huge professional acquaintance with men involved, in one way or another, with art and architecture, often associated with the National Trust as committee members, staff members, advisers or donors [...] including John Betjeman, Anthony Blunt, Kenneth Clark, Alec Clifton-Taylor, David Crawford, Ralph Dutton, Oliver Esher, Robin Fedden, Peter Fleetwood-Hesketh, John Fowler, Derek Hill, George Howard, Christopher Hussey, Wyndham Ketton-Cremer, [...] Paul Methuen, [...] Michael Peto, Michael Rosse, Sachie Sitwell, John Summerson, and Gerry Wellington.

Ralph was most definitely a member of this circle and knew all of these men.

Their influence on British culture was in some ways benign—they undertook research; they were often generous with their time, money and possessions; sometimes they allowed access to their homes and collections; and they wished to educate and entertain. The importance of private individuals in championing the preservation of the nation's heritage cannot be doubted—James Stourton's book *Heritage* cites dozens of examples—but it is also

James Lees-Milne with his wife Alvilde, 1950s

the case that they presided over organisations that were at the time exclusive, exclusionary (no children in the museum, please!), snobbish and clannish. They were more interested in the past than the present, and used the 'natural timeless beauty' of the eighteenth century as justification for sustaining an eighteenth-century social hierarchy, where they, naturally, sat at the top. Kenneth Clark described eighteenth-century England as:

> the paradise of the amateur; by which I mean of men rich enough and grand enough to do whatever they liked, who nevertheless did things that require a good deal of expertise. […] They were independent, with all the advantages and disadvantages to society that result from that condition.

He could have been writing about his own friends.

Several people from Bloch's list (alongside others among Ralph's circle such as Sir Brinsley Ford and the cartoonist Sir Osbert Lancaster) were members of the Society of Dilettanti, a highly exclusive and rarefied club, rather in the manner of the Uffizi Society. It was set up sometime in the 1730s for noblemen and scholars who had undertaken the Grand Tour. Membership is limited to sixty and election is by secret ballot. An induction ceremony is held at Brooks's, Ralph's club in St James's. The society is a charitable body and gives generous grants to galleries, museums and students. Ralph was elected a member in 1955 and regularly attended their meetings thereafter.

In the following year, 1956, Ralph became heavily involved in an effort to save Cams Hall, a Palladian mansion built around 1770, that lies about fifteen miles from Hinton Ampner overlooking Portsmouth Harbour. The house had been requisitioned by the Admiralty during the war and had been badly damaged by an explosion at a nearby ammunition store in 1950. In a sorry state, it was sold but then left to decline, with the roof-leading and many interior features having been stolen. Ralph became an indefatigable letter writer, contacting local and national officials, straining every sinew in an effort to halt the deterioration. His emotional involvement took a toll and he despaired of finding a solution. In fact, largely thanks to his efforts the house was not demolished, and it survived to experience eventual renewal as a business centre in the 1990s.

Although the building and decoration of Hinton was complete, Ralph continued to add to his collections, including, in 1958, an important painting, *The Allegorical Tomb of Charles Sackville, 6th Earl of Dorset*. This work, from 1720, had originally hung in the Duke of Richmond's dining room at Goodwood. Its acquisition shows Ralph spending liberally to add the finishing touches to his project at Hinton.

At this point Ralph's life was settled and his place among the great and the good of the art world was assured. Now approaching the age of sixty, he was a landowner, a public servant and an author. He gave his time, his expertise and his money to good causes both locally and nationally. In Hampshire he was a local worthy and a fixture in the county. He had created at Hinton a personal paradise, which he shared with his friends and also to a degree with the public—the gardens were opened regularly under the National Gardens Scheme, and the house itself could be visited, in the best Georgian tradition, 'by appointment with the Housekeeper'.

As Ralph himself wrote: 'I now looked forward to being free from any major operations on the house for the remainder of my days.' He had achieved his desire to live well in convivial and beautiful surroundings. He had created tranquility. And then disaster struck.

On Sunday, 3rd April 1960, the weather was particularly unpleasant. There was hardly a trace of spring in the countryside, and a strong south-east wind, almost a gale, was blowing beneath a grey, watery sky. After lunch my inclination was to sit by the fire and read the Sunday papers, but this I felt would be self-indulgent, so instead I went out to the woods for a little beneficial manual labour. Seldom was virtue worse rewarded. As I returned across the park an hour and a half later I saw to my surprise a thin column of smoke rising above the trees from a position apparently in front of the house. Could this be a misplaced bonfire I wondered? As I came nearer I suddenly saw through the shrubs of the garden sharp tongues of flame shining brilliantly beyond the bushes. The catastrophe was now obvious: the house was on fire.

Ralph Dutton holds a painting rescued from the fire:
'the worst moment of the disaster'

Chapter Nine:
1960–1967

The damage caused by the fire at Hinton in 1960 was extensive; the house interior was almost completely destroyed. One of the few objects to survive was 'a vast Dresden clock beneath a glass dome, one of my grandmother's unwise purchases'. The library where the fire had started was ruined; the books were fused together and eventually had to be removed with a pickaxe. The drawing room was beyond redemption, along with the entirety of the upstairs bedrooms and attics, but some quick work enabled a party of helpers to get most of Ralph's possessions out of his small sitting room. Photographs in the local press show a disconsolate Ralph ruefully holding a painting that had been saved from the blaze. It took several hours for the fire to be brought fully under control by a team of firemen struggling with an inadequate supply of water.

Ralph spent the night with some neighbours and returned early the following day to assess the damage.

> [This] was for me the worst moment of the disaster. During the fire the general tumult had been so great, the whole situation so improbable that one's feelings were numbed by the noise and bustle, but to see in the morning light the gutted blackened structure with gaping windows through which appeared scenes of unbelievable chaos, of fallen beams, partly destroyed furniture, mutilated books, was bitter indeed. While from the ruins emanated that despairing stench, that one had known all too well in wartime London, of burnt paint and sodden plaster.

*The interior of Hinton Ampner the morning after the fire
with Ralph Dutton on the right*

It was a wretched moment, and the irony of a fire-watcher having his house consumed by fire cannot have helped. But just as in 1939 Ralph had accepted the inevitable and moved out of Hinton with a stoic heart, so now he was undaunted: 'From the moment that it became clear that the house was practically destroyed, I decided that I would rebuild with the minimum delay.'

This was an extraordinarily courageous thing to do. Ralph at this point was sixty-one years old, and the average life expectancy for men in England in 1960 was sixty-seven, so he might have expected to have only a few years in which to enjoy his resurrected house. The scale of the task was immense, and embarking upon it seemed to the author Raymond Mortimer eccentric: 'Will anyone ever again build so elaborate an English mansion? Probably not

I fear, and Mr Dutton will remain the last dilettante to realise such a fantasy.' Moreover, the house and contents were not fully covered by insurance, and Ralph would have to sell income-generating properties in order to meet the capital costs.

But he was single-minded and the decision was made: the architect Trenwith Wills was back at Hinton within twenty-four hours of the fire to discuss plans for reconstruction. One silver lining was that Ralph could rectify the mistakes he had made in his first rebuilding of 1936. The 1960 version of Hinton has ten fewer attic bedrooms, enabling the lowering of a mansard roof, thereby leaving a neater and cleaner external appearance. Ralph had had regrets about retaining some Victorian features of the drawing room in 1936 ('singularly clumsy and coarse'), but this time he was able to align the details of cornicing, plasterwork, fireplaces and the like with the magnificent eighteenth-century outer window frames from the Adelphi that had fortunately survived the fire.

The domestic wing of Hinton had not been so badly damaged; within a few weeks Ralph was able to move into that part of the house, where he lived in two small rooms for the next three years. This time, rebuilding was an easier process than it had been in the immediate postwar years; there was no more rationing, and the relationship between builder and the architect was on this occasion excellent. The main contractor, Edward J. Duffin, wrote later that 'the architects were a delight to work with. As with every builder, we have had our problems with architects and clients, but not on this job. We were paid promptly every month.'

Apart from sourcing features for the rebuild and looking for replacement furnishings, other arrangements had to be made. Some paintings were sent on loan to Southampton City Art Gallery for the duration of the building work; others were lodged with London dealers; some that were beyond repair had to be formally destroyed for insurance and art-historical purposes.

It was a similar story with furniture. Much had been lost, but some pieces could be restored, and this work was done mainly by Ronald Fleming's firm Mann & Fleming—Fleming had gone into partnership with Dolly Mann, one of London's leading decorators, to create the company in 1949.

Ronald Fleming once again advised Ralph on the colours and decorative schemes for the interiors, being brought in at a relatively late stage in 1962, by which time Ralph had already been on a buying spree as Charles O'Brien noted in the magazine *Apollo*:

> The large number of purchase receipts from London dealers testify to three years of intense activity in restoring and replacing his collection. The new purchases show that Dutton acquired examples of the French and Italian decorative arts. He adopted a more critical discipline in the manner of collecting, drawing up precise lists of objects required for each room and carefully planning their arrangement, on occasion resorting to cut-out models to determine the scale of pieces of furniture in their proposed settings.

Once again, Ralph bought the best, an example being the china display cabinets in the corridor outside his bedroom, purchased from an antique dealer in Warwick, that had come from Marlborough House in London and had been owned by Queen Mary. The library was restored almost exactly as it had been, and Ralph was lucky to find a replacement fire surround for the room in an antique shop in Paris. It came with an exalted provenance— it was said to have come from Marie-Antoinette's palace at Saint-Cloud. The dining room was half-destroyed in the fire; the Angelica Kauffman roundels of gods and goddesses were lost but there was sufficient plasterwork remaining so that moulds could be made for a matching reconstruction. In his book *A Hampshire Manor*, Ralph tells us that 'I was lucky enough to find a young artist, Elizabeth Biddulph, who caught the exact sentiment of those small Olympian scenes and the new paintings have the proper eighteenth century flavour. Thus the room returned to its original appearance.'

However, the outcome was not as satisfactory as this account suggests. Elizabeth Biddulph paid an unannounced visit when Ralph was not at home and saw the roundels *in situ*, and wrote to Ralph expressing her dismay at how they had been installed: 'I do hope you understand that it has had a rather distressing effect on us.' She offered to retouch the paintings, but Ralph couldn't face the prospect of more upheaval. He replied to her letter saying that he was sorry to hear of her anguish and that the decorator 'has made it all look as if it had spent years in a London fog. It was all too drastic.' But, he continues,

> I don't know what to say about your suggestion of retouching them. Perhaps if you hold to it strongly the work could be done at the beginning of September when I expect to be away. The dining room is the only room which has given trouble in the decoration. Several people have had a go at it and the result is rather a mess.

The time and effort involved in the rebuild and redecoration, which took three years, did not deflect Ralph from paying attention to other things in his life. He was always affected when his friends experienced difficulty or distress and wrote to them to express his sympathy. In March 1962 Osbert Sitwell replied in a shaky hand:

> My Dear Ralph,
>
> It was most kind of you to write about David [Horner]. For the first few days he was in a very bad way, but in the afternoon of 14th he took a definite turn for the better, I am thankful to say. I haven't been to see him yet because I can't

walk at all owing to gout and rheumatism. The whole thing
has been absolute hell and continues to be so,

Yours ever,

Osbert.

Ralph was equally punctilious when dealing with strangers,
invariably giving a thoughtful, considered response to their enquiries. A Mr E. Z. Stowell of San Antonio, Texas, wrote enclosing
a photo he had taken on a visit to Cothelstone Manor in Devon,
saying that it looked nothing like the description given in Ralph's
book *The English Country House*. Ralph politely pointed out that
his correspondent's driver had taken him not to Cothelstone
Manor but to Cothelstone *Park*.

While major work was going on in the house, Ralph continued to develop the garden, adding statuary, buying plants and
visiting other gardens for inspiration and education. Following a trip to the garden at Sissinghurst, he wrote to its owner
Vita Sackville-West. The relationship between Ralph and Vita
provides a good example of the knotted entanglements among
their circle. Vita was the cousin of Eddy Sackville-West, a fellow member with Ralph of the Uffizi Society at Oxford. She was
married to Harold Nicolson, who was a member of the National
Trust's Historic Buildings Committee in the mid-1940s (as was
Gerald Wellesley). Nicolson's biographer was James Lees-Milne,
who was also Ralph's friend and National Trust colleague. Harold
and Vita acted as witnesses when James and Alvilde Lees-Milne
married, and then Alvilde began an affair with Vita Sackville-West
in 1955. Both Vita and Alvilde were keen gardeners and when
Alvilde published *The Englishman's Garden* in 1983, she invited
Ralph to contribute a chapter on Hinton Ampner, which he did.

Ralph and Vita's exchange of letters concerned a rare plant in
the garden at Sissinghurst:

5 July 1960

The strange plant you saw here is a *puya alpestris*. I have a young plant of it which I hope you will accept. You will real-ise that it will not flower for some years to come and that it will not flower every year even when it has attained maturity. I think it is very nearly hardy, but better keep it away from frost during the winter. Clarence Elliott who discovered it in Chile keeps it in his coal cellar, as he has no greenhouse, but he suggests that it doesn't altogether appreciate this treat-ment. It will of course need potting on and can quite safely spend some time out of doors.

Yours sincerely,

Vita Nicolson.

By 1962 the renovation of the house was nearing completion and Ralph had achieved something momentous. As the historian Adrain Tinniswood says, commenting on the reconstruction: 'The result, which took three years to complete, was a stunningly beau-tiful piece of neo-Regency inside and out. It remains one of the greatest of all post-war country houses.' The first of many maga-zines to feature the rebuild was the Italian magazine *EPOCA* who photographed Hinton for an article in May 1962 titled '*I Grandi Stili: Inghilterra*'.

The expense involved in rebuilding Hinton was enormous and Ralph had to sell some assets including properties at Wick Hill, Chapel Farm, Hartley Wood Farm, Norton Farm, Hartley Park, East Worldham and West Worldham. All his energies and re-sources were concentrated on Hinton and, despite selling property elsewhere, he continued to add land to the Hinton estate, particu-larly when it safeguarded the view from the house. To this end he bought a property in neighbouring Kilmeston in 1963, retaining about 200 acres but selling the unneeded house and garden.

Ralph Dutton with the building contractor Edward J. Duffin (left)
and the Chief Fire Officer Mr Askel (right)

By early 1963 Ralph was once again able to take up full residency. The first thing he did was to throw a party for everyone who had been involved in the restoration, including the local firemen who had extinguished the 1960 blaze and their wives.

Then, in April, he began to entertain, with a succession of weekend visitors through the summer. The visitors' book begins at Easter with Christabel Aberconway and Leslie Hartley in the house. Christabel Abeconway was one of Ralph's closest friends and often acted as a female co-host. She was eight years older than Ralph, a 'renowned social beauty' and a friend to many artists and writers, including H. G. Wells, Somerset Maugham and the Sitwells; in fact her social circle was vast. She had lived with her husband, Henry McLaren, 2nd Baron Aberconway, at Bodnant in North Wales where they nurtured a famous garden, but he died in 1953 and she survived for another twenty-one years, occupying a house in North Audley Street bequeathed to her by the textile magnate and art collector Samuel Courtauld (he also left her Picasso's *Child with a Dove*). Aberconway was a prolific correspondent, but an indifferent writer, her most popular title being *A Dictionary of Cat Lovers*.

Leslie Hartley, or L. P. Hartley as he is better known, was, by contrast, a very popular author, famous for writing *The Go-Between*. Hartley spent much of his time in Venice where he had an apartment and a personal gondolier. Ralph visited him there frequently, as did Osbert Sitwell, Christabel Aberconway and Ralph's Oxford friends Eddy Sackville-West and Lord David Cecil, 'the man Hartley loved', according to Hartley's biographer Adrian Wright. Hartley was a private man and a tragic figure, 'irreparably damaged by childhood trauma' and by the First World War, apparently unable 'to lead a satisfying and happy adult life'.

The visitors' book for the summer of 1963 records many of Ralph's closest friends: Henry and Judy Studholme, Brinsley Ford, Francis and Jane Watson, Ronald Fleming, Charlotte Bonham-Carter, Paul and Muriel Wallraf, James Pope-Hennessy, Hugh Cholmondeley, James and Alvilde Lees-Milne and Geoffrey Houghton-Brown.

Ralph's guests were impressed by the new Hinton. Brinsley Ford wrote an effusive letter of thanks when he got home:

> Without a tasselled canopy over my head I have hardly slept a wink in my primitive camp bed. I do congratulate you on all that you have achieved. You have created a house even more beautiful than it was before, and that is saying a great deal […]. It was a great excitement for me to see Hinton rise again from the ashes, not as a phoenix, which I have always imagined to be a drab bird with feathers like widows' veils but as a peacock. I was dazzled by its plumage […]. Add

Brinsley (later Sir Brinsley) Ford by Martin Yeoman

to all this the pleasure of seeing you so happily installed in so triumphant a setting and I do not think I need say anything more to persuade you how much I enjoyed myself, how grateful I am to you for having me to stay.

James Pope-Hennessy (writing of a later visit) was equally fulsome:

What a perfectly *charming* and comforting weekend that was. I did so greatly enjoy it. If I was given to envying people their lives (which I am not) I would certainly envy yours the most. A number of persons are, or suppose they are, perfectionists, but few take the infinity of trouble to carry this out as you so splendidly do.

Other guests kept it short and sweet: 'With love from us both and very many thanks for such swagger entertainment.'

From the reaction of visitors, it seems that post-conflagration Hinton was even more enjoyable than its previous incarnation. Ralph had improved the look of the exterior and the garden, thrown off the remnants of Victorianism in the interiors, spent lavishly on new decorations and of course no longer faced the problem of rationing when it came to food and drink. It was a time to enjoy himself in his new home, but this was not just self-indulgence. His pleasure in Hinton came partly from sharing it with his guests and more widely.

Ralph re-opened the gardens to the public on 12 May 1963 and every summer thereafter. Sadly, a few years later there were some burglars among the garden visitors. They entered the house and made off with several clocks and Legge family miniatures, together with two important pictures by Orizzonte (the nickname of the Flemish painter Jan Frans van Bloemen, 1662–1749). By sheer fluke, the clocks were recovered when police stopped a suspicious-looking van long after the burglary occurred, but the paintings and miniatures were never recovered.

May 1963 was a very busy month for Ralph. On the 14th, he became a member of the Historic Buildings Council for England, a statutory body that advised government on the preservation of listed and other buildings of architectural or historical significance. He was reappointed in 1967 and was then asked to serve for a further year in 1971, when he was informed that 'it is in fact only your seniority that has inhibited the Minister from suggesting a longer term'.

The accumulation of public appointments and society memberships meant that by the mid-1960s Ralph had four or five meetings a year at each of the National Trust, the Wallace Collection, the National Art Collections Fund, the Historic Buildings Commission, the Hospital of St Cross, the Society of Dilettanti, the Winchester Art Club and the local school where he was a governor.

In addition Ralph continued to write and give speeches to art and historical societies. In 1963 *English Court Life from Henry VII to George II* was published, and then in 1965 came *Sir Christopher Wren*. All through the 1960s, he was in demand as a writer of articles and book reviews for magazines and newspapers. The range of his subjects was broad: examples include articles for issues of the annual *Ideal Home Book* on Hinton Ampner, Broadlands and White Lodge in Richmond (built as a hunting lodge for George II but now the home of the Royal Ballet School); an article on the Valley of the Adour in France for the travel section of the *Glasgow Herald*; and a review of his friend Sacheverell Sitwell's *Monks, Nuns and Monasteries* for *The Times Literary Supplement*.

Despite all this activity he still found time to travel, with trips to the United States in 1964 and 1966, Finland in 1966, East Germany in 1967 and regular visits to France, Belgium, Germany and Italy throughout the decade.

Christopher Hussey, who had written about Hinton Ampner for *Country Life* in 1947 repeated the exercise in 1965 for the 10 June 'Collectors' number'. A colour photograph of Hinton's drawing room with its yellow striped wallpaper and blue/green curtains graced the cover. Hussey judged the new interiors at Hinton to be 'no less, and in some respects more, distinguished' than those of their predecessor:

> The ground-floor rooms reconstructed seem at first sight much as they were but handsomer. Looking more closely, one observes that the changes show a broader appreciation of neo-classical taste in its European as well as its English manifestations. French decorative arts of the 18th century and Italian painting of the 17th now enter more into the Georgian synthesis, reflecting the interests for which Mr Dutton is known both as a writer and as a Trustee of the Wallace Collection.

Hussey's mention of French decorative arts and Italian paintings hits the mark. Ralph had learnt much about the former through his connection with the Wallace Collection, as James Mann, who preceded Francis Watson as director of the Wallace, had noticed when writing to the government about the renewal of Ralph's trusteeship in 1955: 'I think his time here has even influenced his taste. He recently bought a fine clock by Thomire which we would not be ashamed to show.' Mann also comments on Ralph's approach to meetings: 'Though not a great contributor to discussion, what he says is always to the point.' Ralph's expertise in Italian paintings meanwhile was recognised in an article in *Apollo* devoted to his collection.

Ralph was now entering his late sixties, still full of energy, still working, and fully luxuriating in the pleasures of Hinton.

Chapter Ten:
1968–1985

Back in 1926 Ralph had mentioned in his round-the-world travel diary that he might set about writing a history of Hinton. Forty years later he began the task by undertaking detailed investigations into his own genealogy, tracing how Hinton had descended to him through ten generations from Sir Thomas Stewkeley (*c.* 1570–1639) 'who seems to have been the first to live at Hinton Ampner'. The crest of five ostrich feathers that Ralph used as a decorative motif throughout the house and also as an adornment to some of the ceramics that he commissioned, probably dates from a grant of arms to Thomas Stewkeley in 1595, although a more romantic account contained in nineteenth-century copies of *Collins's Peerage* says that the crest was awarded to the Dutton family, along with three other families, by the Black Prince after the battle of Poitiers in 1356.

Ralph's book about Hinton, *A Hampshire Manor*, was published in 1968. Ralph was writing about somewhere that he knew intimately and that he loved. In all important respects, he had created Hinton and the book reflects his knowledge and attachment to the place. *A Hampshire Manor* was a great success and the publisher, Batsford, was delighted. In August 1968 they wrote:

> What a splendid start the book has got off to. Sales have been encouraging too, and so far amount to something like 800 copies. The reviewers for once in a way do seem to have seen the point of the book. I am glad to see that they share our own feelings about it rather than your more modest ones.

Ralph Dutton at his desk at Hinton Ampner, 1983

The reviewers were indeed appreciative. The cricket commentator and journalist John Arlott, himself a Hampshire man, began his fulsome review in the *Hampshire County Magazine* by observing that 'Mr Dutton has built a reputation over the past thirty years as an admirably unsensational writer of accuracy, sensibility and scholarship on English architecture, gardens and topography.' In *Apollo*, the lawyer and novelist Bryan Guinness wrote that Ralph 'speaks with authority and writes with charm and a quiet sense of humour'. But James Lees-Milne, enjoying his own considerable literary success by this time, wrote a rather patronising letter: 'It is a charming little book and marks your crowning contribution to Hinton Ampner's history.'

Another letter then arrived from Batsford: 'You may remember my suggesting we might see whether Robert Harling would be interested in reprinting some of the book in *House and Garden*. He replied this morning at unprecedented speed to the effect that indeed he would.'

Before long, Ralph began to receive fan mail and a stream of letters continued for years. Some must have been welcome, such as that from the historian A. L. Rowse: 'If near here do come to lunch or dine at All Souls.' Others probably amused Ralph: 'My husband is interested in football and cricket in Bramdean [...]'; 'Would you mind signing my copy? [...]'; 'You may remember I got in touch with you a few years ago [...]'; 'It is very seldom that I write to an author but I feel impelled to write to you to say how much I enjoyed it [...]'; and, from New Zealand: 'First of all I should like to mention your command of the English language [...] As for myself, I visited Winchester, with its superb cathedral, in 1955 [...].'

One letter must have been especially welcome. It came from George Speechley, a piano-tuner who had looked after the Broadwood at Hinton for decades:

> In a lifetime of entering the houses of the wealthy I think of Hinton Ampner as being the one most near to perfection. It gave me about as much pleasure as I can ever hope to experience from a house and its contents, and its beauty penetrated my consciousness to the extent that I have never forgotten. Please do not answer my letter Sir, for it is not designed to that purpose. It is that I wish you to know that Hinton Ampner gave to at least one person the very maximum pleasure.

The publication and reception of *A Hampshire Manor* made 1968 a triumphant year for Ralph, but by the winter both he and a number of his friends were beginning to experience the effects of age. In mid-December Ralph had a fall while walking along the terrace to the south of the house and had to go to hospital, where he remained for Christmas.

Christabel Aberconway wrote a letter of commiseration on Christmas Eve:

Dearest Ralph,

Being in my 79th year I no longer send Christmas cards. In place of a Christmas card (most of those I receive have *nothing* to do with the birth of Christ) I am sending you a little book long out of print [the book was one of hers, *The Story of Mr Korah*, illustrated by Rex Whistler]. If I have already given you a copy of this absurd tale hand this one on to your favourite nurse. But ask her to *read* the introduction before turning over the other pages or she will think I am mad (perhaps I am!). Fond love, and I only wish that you were back at Hinton Ampner for Christmas.

Christabel

Osbert Sitwell's secretary also wrote, from Montegufoni:

4/1/69

We were so sorry to hear from Lady Aberconway that you have had a fall and that you have been operated on as a consequence. Sir Osbert would have liked to write to you himself, but he doesn't feel up to dictating letters at present, which he hopes you will understand.

Osbert did not have long to live; he died on 4 May.

Aberconway and Sitwell were both several years older than Ralph, as was Ronald Fleming, who had died in 1968, when Ralph contributed an obituary to *The Times*. Next to go was Gerald Wellesley who passed away aged eighty-six on 4 January 1972, and then it was the turn of L. P. Hartley. James Lees-Milne recorded meeting Ralph at the memorial service:

A and I went to Leslie Hartley's memorial service in Holy Trinity, Brompton. Congregation large, all old friends, most of them with one foot in the grave [...]. Christabel Aberconway, escorted by Ralph Dutton sat beside me. She smelled of gin and talked throughout. Took one of my fingers and said loudly 'Do you remember who I am?'

Ralph's fall took a toll on his general health. One friend wrote calling it 'a catastrophe'; another 'noticed how thin you had got and how little you ate when we had a delicious luncheon with you. As soon as we get back from Mexico we will ring up to see how you are.'

Amid all this death and decline Ralph himself began gradually to relinquish his commitments and to do less. His final book, fittingly enough *Hampshire*, appeared in 1970 to respectful reviews, but it was not in the same league as *A Hampshire Manor.* Although Ralph knew the county well, the narrative skates over the surface, is highly opinionated and borrows heavily from his previous work *Wessex.* It was a wise decision to end his writing career there.

Ralph also began to retire from his life as a trustee and committee man. He stepped down from the Wallace Collection in 1969 and its chairman, the 6th Baron Leconfield and 1st Baron Egremont, who instigated his family's donation of Petworth to the National Trust, wrote a brief latter of thanks 'for all your wise, kind, understanding help and advice over so many years […]. All of us connected with Hertford House will miss you so much.'

In 1972 Ralph ended his association with the Historic Buildings Council, and then in 1973 he retired from one of his most important committees, the Property Committee at the National Trust, as James Lees-Milne records:

> A National Trust dinner at the St James' Club organized by Robin Fedden (who loves these dinners) in honour of Ralph Dutton's retirement on reaching 75. Michael Rosse paid a charming little tribute to Ralph, who murmured that he was too moved to make a speech in reply.

Meanwhile, through all of this, daily life carried on at Hinton and at Ralph's Eaton Square flat. Ralph's godson Henry Legge remembers going with his mother to visit Ralph at the flat, carrying with them a gift of a Derbyshire blue-john object from Asprey's—a present very much to Ralph's liking. The flat was at the top of a long flight of stairs and they were greeted by a kind and generous man, always impeccably dressed and with a mane of sweeping white hair. At the entrance to the flat there was a Boucher-like painting by Casanova's brother. Then they all went off to lunch 'at Claridge's or somewhere like that'.

When he was in London, Ralph cooked and shopped for himself and also went about by public transport, but at Hinton he was fully looked after. The weekend parties continued and distinguished visitors came from time to time. One was Selwyn Lloyd, the speaker of the House of Commons and former chancellor, who came principally to see the gardens in 1971. The next year there was a visit from the Queen who wrote an appreciative note from Windsor Castle on 23 June 1972:

Dear Mr Dutton.

It was such a pleasure to pay you a visit last week, and I greatly enjoyed seeing the lovely garden and your beautiful house so full of treasures—one does not often see a garden so well placed with sudden exquisite views to thrill one, and my own garden looked a positive jungle after your green walks and splendid clumps of shrubs and roses! With warm thanks for your kindness and hospitality,

I am yours sincerely,

Elizabeth R.

Some other visitors were unexpected, but still made to feel welcome. On New Year's Eve 1970 Ralph looked out of the window and noticed two strangers walking around the garden. Instead of chasing them away, he donned an overcoat and took them on a tour of the grounds and the church which lies a few yards from Hinton's front door.

Ralph never commented on his own faith, but he attended services at Hinton and also went to church when he was in Venice. He took a great interest in the fabric of Hinton's All Saints Church. In 1952 he had had two seventeenth-century monuments with Stewkeley family connections moved to Hinton from St Mary's Church, Laverstoke in the north of Hampshire. In the late 1960s he made a number of improvements, including commissioning new east windows from the stained-glass artist Patrick Reyntiens, who had collaborated with John Piper on windows at Coventry Cathedral and Eton College Chapel. Ralph very much approved of these strikingly colourful windows and wrote an appreciative letter to Reyntiens; he also had the windows professionally photographed for him. In addition a new floor and clergy stall were installed in the church. These renovations and additions were celebrated at a service of dedication led by the Bishop of Winchester in September 1970.

Although Ralph stopped writing books in 1970, he nevertheless continued to be busy with articles, book reviews and talks. He also dealt assiduously with correspondence from people seeking information on family genealogy or asking questions arising from his books. Another part of his correspondence concerned the loan of his pictures. In 1973, for example, he lent two paintings by Henry Fuseli to an exhibition organised by the Tate Gallery that then toured to the Hamburger Kunsthalle and the Petit Palais in Paris.

In addition, Ralph was still attending meetings of the few committees where he remained a member. Although reticent and often silent at meetings, Ralph could nonetheless express opinions as decisive as those that appear in his books. In 1973, during a visit to Erddig, a house in Wrexham in Wales that had been offered to the Trust, James Lees-Milne recorded that 'The house itself is barely interesting. Ralph Dutton does not think the place acceptable.'

In fact Erddig went on to become extremely popular and in 2007 it was voted the nation's 'favourite historic house'. Its success derived from the fact that it was the first National Trust property to focus on life downstairs: 'for the first time the staff took centre stage.' This would have been of no interest to Ralph, who was only concerned with the building and the upstairs' contents.

During the mid-1970s, Ralph continued the slow process of making his life simpler. He sold Bramdean Manor, originally purchased for his mother in 1935 and then let after she died in 1946. He continued to make occasional trips to Europe, but no longer to the United States. The year 1977 marked his final withdrawal from committee work with the National Trust, when he stood down from the Gardens Committee, a position where, as he said with typically self-deprecating wit, 'senility can do no harm'. The Trust's chairman, Lord Antrim wrote on 13 May:

> Formally I would like to express my especial thanks to you on behalf of the Trust and to say how deeply the Trust is indebted to you; informally I would like to say with what personal sadness I view the end of this long association, and also to add how much the staff, whose respect and affection you long ago won, are going to miss you.

Then in 1979 Ralph had a rejuvenating trip to Venice. Older people often take pleasure in introducing the younger generation to those things in life that they enjoy, passing on experiences and accumulated knowledge, and in that way they relive their own youth. So it was with Ralph. At some point, though we do not know exactly how or when, he met an American actor called Bradford Garnett and, in the spring of 1979, when Ralph was seventy-nine and Brad thirty, they went together to Venice. Brad wrote an account of the trip and sent a copy to Ralph. The writing style is reminiscent of a Regency novel:

> Before long I recognised the approach of the house, and the familiar sight produced that singular joy associated with seeing my great friend. Ralph greeted me in the hall and soon we were in the library, where with refreshments in hand we exchanged news. There began two blissful days of quiet fraternity before we embarked for Venice.

Once there they settled into their respective rooms at the Hotel Europa on the Grand Canal opposite the Salute; they went straight to Harry's Bar, where Ralph was well known and warmly greeted by the proprietor. Ralph was also recognised by the barber at the Hotel Bauer Grünwald, even though he hadn't been there for six years.

While in Venice they visited Ralph's old friends Paul and Muriel Wallraf—Ralph had spent many Christmases with them at their apartment in the Ca' Malipiero in Campo Maria Formosa—and also called on the aged Princess Clary: 'Ralph informed this Yankee that he would get to meet a genuine German Princess.' Ralph was very well-connected in Venice and his address book contains the names of notable Venetian residents and Venice aficionados such as Peggy Guggenheim and John Julius Norwich.

Together Brad and Ralph were indefatigable sightseers:

> Ralph noted at dinner that we had walked very nearly from one end of Venice to the other, and its breadth as well. His fatigued companion did not dispute this calculation. It did not fail to impress me that Ralph, a man fifty years my senior, was no worse for wear having matched me step for step.

When they went to St George's, the Anglican church, on Sunday, Ralph was recognised by the man who read the lesson, the American author Peter Lauritzen, who had written several authoritative books about Venice. Lauritzen invited them for cocktails but the event turned out to be more than they expected, with Ralph 'the guest of honour'. Brad managed to rescue him 'so that we might leave the party after an acceptable stay of about 60 minutes'.

It is clear from Brad's account that he, like Ralph, preferred privacy and quiet. One evening, a couple from Memphis, occupying the table next to theirs at dinner, started talking to them:

> Ever courteous, Ralph was cordial to my compatriots, which charmed them. Fortunately they were not overbearing, possibly because they sensed we were really a quiet pair. Later I was amused by Ralph's description of the incident: 'chat but no frat.'

Ralph and Brad remained friends and when Brad married in 1984, he and his new wife honeymooned in Venice. This prompted Brad to revisit his account of their trip: 'I have re-read it a number of times recently, to bone up, and each reading has wrought a tremendous sense of debt for your tutelage. I hope you recognize this feeling occasionally.' Brad stayed in touch with both Ralph and his sister Joane and was able to revisit Hinton.

After the Venice trip, Ralph returned to Hinton via Paris, but later in 1979 his notebooks show a sudden change in his handwriting, indicating a severe deterioration of some sort. The elegant copperplate is replaced by capital letters that appear to be written with effort. The explanation may be that Ralph's eyesight, never good, had rapidly worsened.

When James Lees-Milne met Ralph he commented on the problem: 'Lunched with dear old Ralph Dutton and Geoffrey

Houghton-Brown at Grosvenor Hotel. Ralph is extremely blind; cannot read more than headlines of newspapers, yet will not try to get a really potent magnifying glass.' A letter to Ralph from a helpful Eaton Square neighbour around the same time provides details about the National Listening Library (a postal audiobook library service). Ralph must have appreciated the contact, because he made great use of the library and left them a legacy of £1,000. Brinsley Ford also helped, by reading aloud to Ralph at Hinton.

For the last four years of his life Ralph unexpectedly enjoyed a new status as a peer. In 1982 he inherited the title of 8th Baron Sherborne from a distant younger cousin—they shared a common ancestor in Ralph's great-grandfather John Dutton (1779–1862), the 2nd Baron Sherborne. The historian R. C. Richardson, who interviewed Ralph's housekeeper in her later years says that 'He rejoiced in his elevation to the peerage and, in truth, became something of a snob; he relished the way in which he was locally revered and insisted on being addressed by his new title.'

The title came up in conversation during both of the last two occasions that James Lees-Milne saw Ralph, in February and December 1984:

> London Library all morning. Walked to Eaton Square and lunched with dear Ralph Dutton. He asked me to read out a letter he had just received from Geoffrey Houghton-Brown. Can't see to read the newspaper headlines, let alone letters. But in excellent form and absolutely *compos*. Said he had taken his seat in the House of Lords, being led up to the woolsack and prompted when to bow to Hailsham. Then led out of the chamber.

and

> Geoffrey Houghton-Brown and Ralph Dutton lunched. Geoffrey is thin in face but otherwise unchanged [...] Ralph also older, his nose larger than ever. The dearest man. Says

how now he is a Lord people are more deferential, and like working for him. But he gets begging letters daily because Charles Sherborne left an estate valued at £6 million, though not a penny to him. We lunched at the Grosvenor Hotel where G. M. Trevelyan used to take me between N.T. meetings. He never tipped the waiter more than sixpence.

Ralph's final will was made in March 1983 and the main disposition was to bequeath Hinton Ampner, together with almost all its contents and a substantial endowment to the National Trust. The decision to make this extraordinarily generous gift had been taken in the early 1960s after the second rebuild of the house, when Ralph wrote a short letter to Michael Rosse, then chairman of the Trust, stating his intentions. Ralph did not impose any conditions, nevertheless the arrival of the letter caused some consternation. It was difficult to look this gift-horse in the mouth, and yet there was a constituency among the National Trust who thought that while the garden and landscape were outstanding, the house was too modern—and therefore of insufficient merit— to accept. There were also concerns that the endowment might not be enough to support the opening of the house.

These reservations were not communicated to Ralph and matters were left in abeyance until the mid-1980s, when Ralph's devoted sister Joane, to whom he was very close, and some of his friends made it clear that they thought Ralph should find out exactly what the Trust intended to do.

Ralph asked one of his lawyers to undertake the task of negotiating with the National Trust. A response came from the Trust's Property Committee to the effect that they gratefully accepted his gift, but planned to let the house to a tenant, albeit with public access to the garden and the downstairs rooms for the summer months. Not surprisingly this upset Ralph very much.

His lawyer protested, but before any action could be considered Ralph died, on Saturday 20 April 1985, after falling down the staircase at Hinton following a serious bout of pneumonia. 'Considerate and well-mannered to the end, he waved to the faithful Mrs Cross [the cook] as he was carried on a stretcher to a waiting ambulance.'

The funeral service was held at All Saints, Hinton Ampner, on Friday 10 May 1985, and the weather was appropriate to the occasion: cold, overcast and drizzly. It was a traditional service with the congregation singing 'Lead kindly Light', 'He who would valiant be' and 'The day thou gavest, Lord, is ended'. The readings were from Ecclesiastes, chapter 11: 'The light of the day is sweet, and pleasant to the eye is the sight of the sun; if a man lives for many years, he should rejoice in all of them.'

Ralph had led a civilised life in turbulent times; he had made the most of his long years and he had indeed rejoiced in them.

Epilogue

Two obituaries of Ralph Dutton appeared in the press. In *The Times*, Sir Brinsley Ford gave a factual summary of the events of Ralph's life, but in the *Hampshire Chronicle* Ralph's friend and Alresford neighbour, Ralph Ricketts wrote a more emotional and personal account, noting Ralph's generosity, and also saying that:

> He was a sympathetic listener, and beneath his fastidious but kindly manner concealed a real humility and a complete absence of any form of malice. Lord Sherborne was a brave man. He accepted his increasing blindness with courage and even with humour. He set himself a high standard which he lived up to in an increasingly vulgar world, and will be missed by his friends from all walks of life, not least by his tenants, estate workers, and household staff.

Ralph undoubtedly possessed the virtues of an Edwardian gentleman: he was kind, generous, gentle, understated and public-spirited. He was stoic and uncomplaining in the face of adversity, refusing to fuss or feel sorry for himself and, when faced with setbacks, he was resilient, not least when it appeared that Hinton had been destroyed by fire. He was cultured, stylish and elegant. He had a strong attachment to his home and his county, yet he was a cosmopolitan Englishman who spoke several languages and was at home in the wider world, especially the cultured worlds of France and Italy.

Ralph's real significance is to be found not in his personality but in his two-fold achievements. First, he played an important role in the rehabilitation of eighteenth-century architecture and design, a change in taste that went on to influence British culture in the mid- and late twentieth century. His life and work also provide an example of how culture itself develops and changes, through the operation of networks of friends, committees and organisations.

Secondly, he conceived and then created at Hinton an idealised life for himself that benefited his friends and the wider public, and from which it is still possible to draw lessons today. The elements of that life included friendship, scholarship, public service and the pleasures of good food, wine, clothes and cars. They involved keeping busy with work and enjoying the stimulus of travel, appreciating fine paintings and *objets d'art*, and cultivating knowledge about everything from trees and flowers to ceramics and drawings.

In 1974 Ralph was interviewed for a BBC Radio Solent programme about the village of Hinton Ampner. His soft, gentle and beautifully modulated voice has a number of quirks. Great becomes 'gwate', as in 'there are a gwate many Hintons'. Corruption becomes 'cowwuption' and century, 'sentchway'. Roundheads are 'Wowndheads'. His language harks back to an earlier era: 'my grandfather inherited this nice Georgian house which was very much out of fashion; it wasn't at all the thing.' Throughout the interview he is a master of understatement; speaking about the devastating events of 1960, he nonchalantly says that 'The house caught fah [...] It wreally was rather heartbreaking.'

More revealingly, he speaks about the community of Hinton:

> I love this village and I think we are a very very happy community. If you have a biggish house, and this is rather a big house, it should be important to the village, and I think it

is here. The people in the village know the house as well as I do, and I think that is a very important thing [...]. I really know everybody in the village. I know the children, and everybody else. I've known them all their lives [...]. We are a very friendly community.

It is true that Ralph was kind and generous to his community. He contributed time and money to local causes and the local school and despite his natural reticence, he engaged with the people around him. He often went out of his way to be helpful: the son of Gladys Trickle (who worked for Ralph and was a church-warden at All Saints), remembered him as a 'firm but encouraging father figure'. Christmases at Hinton were celebrated as great estate occasions with a large party and presents for all the children.

As master of the estate, Ralph created not just a neo-Georgian house, but also a set of neo-Georgian social relationships and hierarchies. However benign those might be both in his imagination and in fact, Ralph's view from the top sounds childlike in its simplicity. As the critic and poet Clive James noted: 'Power is bound to sound naïve because it doesn't spot the bitter nuances of feeling helpless.'

In a similar manner, in their voluntary and professional roles, Ralph's group of friends decided the fate of public bodies, charities and private houses with self-belief, confidence and as of right. They were an exclusive clique who, with very few exceptions, gained entry through birth, and most of them never had to earn a living. Having said that, they worked hard, and it is they who rescued the English country house from what looked at the time like oblivion (Ralph's own view was that the country house would cease to exist not because of taxation but because of a lack of servants). All through the twentieth century, a small group laboured to study and preserve the nation's built heritage. Until 1974, when the Victoria and Albert Museum's exhibition *The Destruction of the*

Country House 1875–1975 cast a bright light on the issue, official-dom and the general public were indifferent to the fate of country houses, but the flame had been kept alive by Ralph and his ilk.

James Lees-Milne described a gathering of their clan:

> What makes them so conspicuous? Not so much their breeding or their appearance, rather their money and secu-rity. Their physical comfort and lack of financial worry leads to self-confidence, sophistication, good taste, in many cases a knowledge of the arts. It also explains their good manners, tolerance, iconoclastic brand of humour, self-deprecation, and willingness to accept those outsiders wishing to be re-ceived whose manners make them acceptable. They are for the most part kindly and compassionate—yet withal proud. They won't admit to being superior, yet consider themselves so. Their society is undoubtedly agreeable, and it is possible for intellectuals to bask in it without being corrupted by their *train de vie*.

There is a traceable thread from the tastes and preferences of this group, validated and promoted through their roles in public institutions, into the wider culture. The starting point is an observation made by the architectural historian Mark Girouard in the 1985 exhibition catalogue *The Treasure Houses of Britain*, where, commenting on the history of the English country house, he says that: 'An independent, property-owning landed class was seen as the right and natural ruling class, but their power and privileges were recognised as bringing corresponding duties.' In the twentieth century, one of those duties was serving on the boards of public organisations. Here, as the cultural historian Robert Hewison points out:

> We like to think of our great cultural institutions as some-how neutral, mere facilities for the presentation of individual

acts of creation, yet they profoundly affect our perception of what is judged to be history or art. As institutions they help to form the culture which they are assumed merely to reflect.

He goes on to say that: 'The specific tastes of a caste or profession are generalised into the tastes of the organisation whose judgements define the official parameters of art.'

Writing in *The Times Literary Supplement* in 1952, Ralph could note with some satisfaction the shift in taste that he and his friends had brought about:

> As recently as the twenties of this century, public interest in the architecture of the Georgian era was still undeveloped. There were enthusiasts, but the general attitude to Georgian building was negative; it was not particularly disliked, but at the same time it was seldom looked on as anything worthy of preservation. This attitude is now rare, and Georgian architecture has almost as good a chance of being treated with respect as examples of the Elizabethan or Jacobean ages.

By the time Ralph died in 1985, Georgian style was widely embraced, and with enthusiasm. The immensely influential TV serialisation of Evelyn Waugh's *Brideshead Revisited* in 1981 had spurred popular enthusiasm for the era and for the cult of the country house in general. 'The Treasure Houses of Britain' exhibition in Washington DC in 1985/86 did similar service in the United States. And both, of course, reflected and encouraged the desire for a change to a more deferential and hierarchical society after the turbulence of the 1960s and 1970s. The reaction to that revisionism, in the form of strikes and riots, were also, in their own way, a revisitation of an eighteenth-century approach, as was the risk-taking buccaneering adventurism adopted in the City of London.

The æsthetic and cultural choices made by Ralph and his close-knit group of friends, who influenced taste-making through the National Trust, *Country Life* and the boards and committees of museums and galleries, had unpredictable consequences that stretched well beyond matters of art and design—though Ralph and his friends would probably have thought it impertinent to say so, and would have seen art and politics as occupying completely separate realms.

In the private sphere, Ralph's enthusiasm for the eighteenth century was tempered by his delight in twentieth-century comforts. Hinton is not a Georgian house; Ralph could have bought one but he preferred to recreate the spirit of the eighteenth century, complete with electricity and bathrooms. He did not want either the genuine article or a slavish imitation obsessed with authentic paint colours; instead Hinton is Ralph's own interpretation of eighteenth-century ideals, both in its æsthetic and in its pursuit of the good life.

Ralph used the wealth that he had inherited to create at Hinton his own romanticised version of life, where everything was of the best, everything was beautiful and everything, personal relationships included, was as congenial as possible. Many people inherit wealth and privilege but few use it to such effect. It must be stressed how unusual Ralph was in building Hinton in the 1930s. Between 1918 and 1945, 485 country houses were demolished, and a further 250 were destroyed after 1945. Ralph's decision to build—and then to rebuild—was a contrarian and courageous act in the face of what looked like the end of a uniquely English cultural creation and tradition. The fact that he then gave Hinton, one of the best country houses of the twentieth century, to the National Trust for the benefit of the public is to be lauded and celebrated.

In his private and working life, Ralph lived up to two ideals; one was the seventeenth-century gentleman, as described by

Harold Nicolson: 'the gentleman was supposed to be considerate to others, to avoid courtly fashions, to spend most of his time on his estates, and to possess, in addition to humility, tolerance, forgiveness and compassion. These are the precious components of true civility.' The other was set out by Ralph's friend David Cecil: 'The Renaissance ideal of the whole man, whose aspiration is to make the most of every advantage, intellectual and sensual, that life has to offer.' In Ralph's case, this has to be tempered with an observation from Kenko, a fourteenth-century Japanese Buddhist monk: 'A man may excel at everything else, but if he has no taste for lovemaking, one feels there is something terribly inadequate about him.' Celibacy that does not stem from religious precept suggests a lack of self-confidence. The novelist Brigid Brophy wrote in the *New Statesman* in 1962 that 'the two most fascinating subjects in the universe are sex and the eighteenth century'; Ralph would have agreed about the second, but who knows what he thought about the first? It would be impolite to ask.

Ralph's approach to life, and to Hinton, was consistent. Each part was designed to blend with, support and harmonise with the other parts. The appreciation of Hinton as an integrated whole, made up of the 1650-acre estate, the house plus its contents, and the garden with its landscape views, is a relatively recent development, but over the past forty years there has been a growing recognition that each aspect of Hinton can only be understood in the context of every other part.

Over the last twenty years the National Trust has widened public access to Hinton Ampner. The house is no longer tenanted and is now open most of the year for visitors to enjoy the collections and interiors. The gardens are likewise open and the traditional National Trust café and shop have been established in some of the outbuildings. The wider estate attracts more than 200,000 walkers. Visitors often comment on the sense of harmony and peace that Hinton gives them. The great American decorator Nancy Lancaster said that when entering a room one should simultaneously be stimulated and soothed, and Hinton Ampner achieves this not just in its interiors but throughout the property.

When Bryan Guinness wrote a review of Ralph's *A Hampshire Manor* for *Apollo*, he concluded that:

> Mr Dutton is to be congratulated on his life's work. How few of us have so thoroughly followed the wisdom of Candide's concluding advice to cultivate our own gardens? Mr Dutton's garden in the wider sense comprehends not only his house and landscape but the human and scholarly that he has expressed in them.

Ralph Dutton devoted his life to building Hinton, designing its garden and furnishing its interiors. He revelled in the rounded and pleasurable life that he had created both there and in London. The last word goes to Cynthia Gladwyn (wife of the diplomat and statesman Lord Gladwyn), who recorded those pleasures in her diary for 16 July 1969:

> Lunched with Ralph Dutton. The form never varies [...]. In the flat, full of choice objects, we have double martinis, and then go to the Coq d'Or and have an excellent lunch of fish and white wine. After which we go to look at pictures in Sotheby's or Christie's, or to an antique shop where he often buys something at a high price. He has nobody but himself to consider, and his Hampshire house and its contents constitute the pleasure of his life. Much of the house was destroyed in a dreadful fire some years ago, but he rebuilt it even more to his liking and has had all the fun of buying more beautiful pictures and furniture.

As the Greek philosopher Epicurus wisely observed: 'It is not what we have, but what we *enjoy* that constitutes our abundance.'

To the Memory of
RALPH STAWELL
DUTTON
8th Baron Sherborne
of
Hinton Ampner House
Born 25th August 1898
Died 20th April 1985

The last of his line

Ralph Dutton's gravestone in All Saints, Hinton Ampner

Bibliography and Sources

Aberconway, C., *A Wiser Woman* (Hutchinson, London, 1966)

Agar, A., *Footprints in the Sea* (Evans Bros, London, 1959)

Annan, N., *Our Age: Portrait of a Generation* (Weidenfeld & Nicolson, London, 1990)

Eton Chronicle, June 1915, July 1915, May 1917

Eton School Register, Part VIII 1908–1919 at https://www.greatwarforum. org/topic/226226, accessed 13/7/2022

'Hinton Ampner House', *Antique Collector*, April 1967, pp. 54-65

'Un Manoir de Goût Anglais', *Connaissance des Arts*, May 1957

'I Grandi Stili: Inghilterra', *EPOCA*, 20 May 1962

The Singapore Free Press, 16 May 1931

Barnes, J., *The Man in the Red Coat* (Jonathan Cape, London, 2019)

— *Letters From London* (Picador, London, 1995)

Battersby, M., *The Decorative Twenties* (Studio Vista, London, 1969)

Berthon, S., *Allies at War: The Bitter Rivalry Among Churchill, Roosevelt and De Gaulle*, (Carroll & Graf, New York, 2001)

Bloch, M., *Closet Queens, Some 20th Century British Politicians* (Little, Brown, London, 2015)

— *James Lees-Milne, The Life* (John Murray, London, 2009)

Bradford, S., *Sacheverell Sitwell; Splendours and Miseries* (Sinclair-Stevenson, London, 1983)

Carpenter, H., *The Brideshead Generation* (Weidenfeld & Nicolson, London, 1989)

Clark, K., *Civilisation* (BBC, London, 1969)

Collard, F., 'The Regency Revival' in *The Journal of the Decorative Arts Society 1890–1940*, 1984, no. 8 (1984), pp. 7–18

Collins, D., *Charmed Life: The Phenomenal World of Philip Sassoon* (William Collins, London, 2016)

Cook, M., *Queer Domesticities: Homosexuality and Home Life in Twentieth Century London* (Palgrave Macmillan, London, 2014)

Cornforth, J., *The Inspiration of the Past* (Viking, London, 1985)
— 'Country House Enthusiasms, Christopher and Betty Hussey's
    Visiting Albums 1936–1970', *Country Life*, 26 January 1984
Cranborne, H. (ed.), *David Cecil, A Portrait by His Friends* (Dovecote
    Press, Wimborne, 1990)
Crombie, T., 'Eighteenth Century Italian Paintings in the Collection
    of Mr Ralph Dutton', *Apollo*, March 1963, pp. 218–21
Dalrymple, W., *White Mughals: Love and Betrayal in 18th-century India*
    (HarperCollins, London, 2002)
Dutton, R., 'Hinton Ampner' in *The Daily Mail Ideal Home Book*, n.d.
    c. 1951/2
— Review of *Looking for Georgian England* by Raymond Francis in
    The Times Literary Supplement, 24 May 1955
— *The English Country House* (Batsford, London, 1935)
— *The English Garden* (Batsford, London, 1937)
— *Wessex* (Batsford, London, 1950)
— *The Victorian Home* (Batsford, London, 1954)
— *A Hampshire Manor* (Batsford, London, 1968)
— *Hampshire* (Batsford, London, 1970)
— Obituary of Lord Holden, *The Times*, 9 July 1951
Eade, P., *Evelyn Waugh: A Life Revisited* (Weidenfeld & Nicolson,
    London, 2016)
Eden, A., *Another World 1897–1917* (Allen Lane, London, 1976)
Elliott, B., 'Historical Revivalism in the Twentieth Century',
    Garden History, 'Reviewing the Twentieth-Century Landscape,'
    28 January 2000
Fenwick, S., *The Crichel Boys*, (Constable, London 2021)
Girouard, M., 'The Power House', in *The Treasure Houses of Britain*,
    ed. G. Jackson-Stops, pp. 22–27 (Yale University Press, New Haven
    and London, 1985)
Heffer, S., (ed) *Henry 'Chips' Channon, The Diaries, vol. 1 1918-38;
    vol. 2 1938-43; vol. 3 1943-57* (Hutchinson, London, 2021-22)
Hewison, R., *The Heritage Industry* (Methuen, London, 1987)
Hind, C., 'Sound and Fury—the Early Days of the Georgian Group',
    The Georgian Group Report and Journal, 1986, pp. 45–54
Hussey, C., 'Hinton Ampner House, Hampshire', *Country Life*, 7 and
    14 February 1947, and 10 June 1965
— 'Those Were the Days', *Country Life*, 25 July 1947, pp. 176–77

— *English Country Houses: Early Georgian, Mid Georgian, Late Georgian* (3 vols) (Country Life, London 1955/1956/1958)

Keel, T., 'Hinton Ampner', *Country Life*, 20 October 2018

Kenko, *Essays in Idleness*, trans. Meredith McKinney (Penguin Classics, London, 2013)

Jackson, S., *The Sassoons* (Heinemann, London, 1968)

James, C., *Cultural Amnesia* (Picador, London, 2008)

Jebb, M. (ed.), *The Diaries of Cynthia Gladwyn* (Constable, London, 1995)

Jourdain, M., *Regency Furniture 1795–1820*, (Country Life, London, 1934)

— 'Ralph Dutton's Collection of Regency Furniture', *Country Life*, London, 6 December 1946

Lancaster, O., *Homes Sweet Homes*, (John Murray, London, 1946 [1939])

Langford, S., *Rotted, Stories of Life, Land and a Farming Revolution* (Viking, London, 2022)

Lees-Milne, A. and R. Verey, *The Englishman's Garden* (Allen Lane, London, 1982)

Lees-Milne, J., *Harold Nicolson, a biography*, vols. 1 and 2, (Chatto & Windus, London, 1980-81)

— *Fourteen Friends* (John Murray, London, 1996)

— *Ancient as The Hills, Diaries 1973–74* (John Murray, London, 1997)

— *Deep Romantic Chasm Diaries 1979–81* (John Murray, London, 2000)

— *Holy Dread, Diaries 1982–84* (John Murray, London, 2001)

— *Beneath a Waning Moon, Diaries 1985–87* (John Murray, London, 2003)

Leslie, S., *The End of a Chapter* (Constable, London, 1916)

Levy, M., 'From Thomas Hope to Vogue Regency and beyond: the growing appreciation of Regency design during the twentieth century', *Regency Furniture and Works of Art*, H. Blairman & Sons, 2020, https://blairman.co.uk/wp-content/uploads/2020/02/Blairman-Regency-Furniture-and-Works-of-Art.pdf, accessed 17 April 2023.

Mosley, C. (ed), *The Letters of Nancy Mitford and Evelyn Waugh* (Hodder & Stoughton, London, 1996)

National Trust, *Hinton Ampner* (National Trust, London, 1988)

— *Hinton Ampner* (National Trust, Swindon, 2020)

— *Hinton Ampner Garden* (National Trust, Swindon, 2000)

— *National Trust Magazine*, Spring 1996

Nichols, B., *Merry Hall* (Jonathan Cape, London, 1951)

Nichols, B., *The Unforgiving Minute* (W. H. Allen, London, 1978)

Nicolson, H., *Good Behaviour* (Constable, London, 1955)

O'Brien, C., 'Ralph Dutton and Ronald Fleming at Hinton Ampner House', *Apollo*, no. 422, 1997, pp. 43–47

Pearson, G., *Hooligan, A History of Respectable Fears* (Macmillan, London, 1983)

Powers, A., 'Ronald Fleming and Vogue Regency', *The Journal of the Decorative Arts Society*, no. 19, 1995, pp. 51–58

Pryce-Jones, A., *The Bonus of Laughter* (Hamish Hamilton, London, 1987)

Rhodes James, R., *Anthony Eden* (Weidenfeld & Nicolson, London, 1986)

Richardson, R.C., '"Englishness" and Heritage: Ralph Dutton (1898-1985), 8th Lord Sherborne, and Hinton Ampner, Hampshire' in *Social History, Local History and Historiography* (Cambridge Scholars Publishing, Newcastle on Tyne, 2011)

Richardson, T., *English Gardens in the Twentieth Century* (Aurum Press, London, 2005)

Robinson, J. M., *The Latest Country Houses* (Bodley Head, London, 1984)

Roper, L., 'A Notable Modern Garden', *Country Life,* 19 September 1957

Russell, E. (ed.), *A Constant Heart, The War Diaries of Maud Russell 1938-1945* (The Dovecote Press, Wimborne Minster, 2017)

Sales, J., '"All the Running you can do": Hinton Ampner Garden, Hampshire', *Country Life*, 14 May 1987

Sitwell, O., Interview in *Time* magazine, 30 September 1966

Sitwell, S., *Conversation Pieces* (Batsford, London, 1936)

Sotheby's, *The Dutton Family by John Zoffany* (Sotheby's, London, 2001)

Stourton, J., *Heritage* (Head of Zeus, London, 2022)

Thwaite, A. (ed), *My Oxford* (Robson Books, London, 1977)

Tinniswood, A., *The House Party: A Short History of Leisure, Pleasure and the Country House Weekend* (Faber and Faber, London, 2019)

Tinniswood, A., *Noble Ambitions* (Jonathan Cape, London, 2021)

Waterson, M., *A Noble Thing: The National Trust and its Benefactors* (Scala, London, 2011)

Wood, M., *Nancy Lancaster* (Francis Lincoln, London, 2005)

Wright, A., *Foreign Country: The Life of L. P. Hartley* (Andre Deutsch, London, 1996)

Ziegler, P., *Osbert Sitwell* (Chatto & Windus, London, 1998)

websites:
https://www.mymaughamcollection.com/p/home.html, accessed 17
    April 2023
http://www.jamesleesmilne.com, accessed 17 April 2023

Picture credits

Pages 1 and 4: author; page 2: Henry Burrows via Flickr; pages 10, 16, 19, 20, 21, 34, 71, 75, 100, 124 and 131: © National Trust Images; page 12: © National Trust Images/Hugh Mothersole; pages 14, 29, 32, 33, 55, 63 and 73: Wikimedia Commons; page 23: Bonhams; page 27: TuckDB Postcards; page 38: Thanks to Mirabel Cecil, Alamy; page 45: Library of Congress; page 48: publisher's collection; page 50: Thanks to Clare Hastings for permission; page 52: Sotheby's; page 59: Robert Nate via Flickr; page 66: Gooding & Co; pages 76 and 77: © National Trust Images/Charles Thomas; page 80: Unknown photographer, author's collection; page 86: Thanks to Portsmouth High School GDST for permission; page 97: © National Trust Images/Nick Carter; page 111: Thanks to Wallace Collection for permission; page 113: Beinecke Library, Yale; pages 116 and 118: Thanks to Hampshire Chronicle for permission; page 126: Thanks to Martin Yeoman (sculptor) and Prudence Cuming Associates Limited (photographer) for permission; page 151: LordHarris [sic], Wikipedia

Index

First published 2023 by
Pallas Athene (Publishers) Limited,
2 Birch Close, London N19 5XD

www.pallasathene.co.uk

© Pallas Athene 2023

Text copyright © John Holden 2023

The right of John Holden to be identified as the author
of this work has been asserted in accordance with the
Copyright Designs and Patents Act 1988

All rights reserved. Except for brief quotations in a review,
this book, or any part thereof, may not be reproduced, stored
in or introduced into a retrieval system, or transmitted, in
any form by any means, electonic, mechanical photocopying,
recording or otherwise, without the prior written permission
of the publisher.

Cover photograph © Derry Moore

ISBN 978 1 84368 239 4

Printed in England

 @pallasathenebooks   @PallasAtheneBooks

 @Pallas_books   @Pallasathene0